Steve Perry

Man up!
Nobody is coming to
save us

A Renegade Book

Middletown CT USA

Cover design: by Quick-E Sign & Copy
Cromwell & Middletown, CT

Front cover photo features the Greensboro Four: Franklin McCain, Joseph McNeil, Ezell Blair, Jr. and David Richmond in 1960 sit in at a N.C. Woolworth. All were attending North Carolina A&T.

Back cover features Steve Perry at The Russel on Pratt Street in 2005 in Hartford , CT Photo by Roxanne Williams

Printed and published by:
Renegade Books
40 Middlefield Street
Middletown, Connecticut 06457

Printed in Three Rivers, MA in the United States of America

ISBN: 0-9708929-2-6

Shout outs, big ups and thanks

Big ups to my wife. This book has been a bear. It's done. No one has given more than you to me. Thank you.

Mason and Walker, my two sons, you inspire me. You make me want to be there for those boys who won't have their father read to them tonight. Your blessings remind me that so many little boys are starved for the complexity and comfort of a father/son relationship. So please understand that when I am not with you it is because I want to share the love that we have for each other with those kids. Please know that there is nothing that you do that is insignificant to me. And please understand that no matter where the inspiration of our relationship takes me, that every breath you take, every vow you break, I'll be watching you.

Mom, thanks for making it all make sense. Now we'll wait for everyone else to catch up.

Daddy, things are looking up for us and you're the reason why. Thank you for proving that a man can change. This is the greatest lesson that I have ever learned.

To my crew, Kenny, Cle, Fult, Rich, Baye, and G, good lookin' out fellas. You have propped me up and kept me grounded. Then, when it all seems impossible, you show me that it's not.

To my team, Roxanne and Flor, though it's been 7 years and 100% of our kids have made it to college, we're just getting started. Thank you for your devotion. It's what the kids needed and more than I deserve.

Lehronda Upshur and the Power 99 family, thanks for always making Philly feel like home. Authors and friends Brenda L. Thomas, Vincent Alexandria and all of the Brother 2 Brother authors, thanks for your support and inspiration.

To all my kids and families at the Capital Preparatory Magnet School and ConnCAP, your unmatched drive and willingness to grow shows me that even with a man like me, something as beautiful as our little school can be born.

Brother 'Suf, you have been the spirit of this book. When they come after me I'm sending them to come get you.

We can do it

This book is a gut check. It explores what happens when we don't use our resources to save ourselves. Then it looks at what needs to be done by both Black men and women to save Black men and by extension, our community.

The most important point in this book is that Black people have the ability and resources to completely alter our condition. I highlight basic strategies that have or could move us forward. Every single one of us has talents and gifts. This book is suggesting that if more of us use them more strategically, the Black condition will forever improve.

I live in the future because I work with children everyday. I am the principal and a founder of an inner city magnet middle and high school. With each rising of the sun I am confronted with a painful reality. Our Black boys are in tremendous trouble.

It is irrefutable that our boys' school performances are dead last among all racial groups. The question is why. It is easy to pin their underperformance on White racism. It is also an incomplete assessment.

Traditionally we begin and end our search into what is wrong in the Black community with pointing an angry injured finger at White people and *the system*. Both are easy targets because the accusation has historical foundations.

Unearthing the ghosts of White people's past, present and future does not complete our understanding of why the Black condition persists in education or industry. When we blame them, we are expunged of responsibility for the condition of Black people. This allows us to occupy the peculiar position of victim.

Fortunately the answers that we seek are much more complicated than 'blaming The Man.' It is good for Black folks to know that there are flaws in the assumptions that the root of all Black problems is White people. It is downright freeing to know that we have a hand in perpetuating our current condition. That also means that we can fix it.

Black people are at the helm of many of the systems that impact our lives today. We raise, entertain, feed, lead and educate our children. Failure to own our role in the creation of the condition of our community robs us of the chance to improve it. Once we recognize that we, more than any other group, have the power to transform our currently deplorable circumstances. We will finally take hold of the opportunity to foster a healthy Black community.

Man Up! was written to shine the light on us all. The issues that our boys face are so pronounced that we all must take responsibility for solving them. We can't depend on other groups to be our scapegoats or saviors anymore. All of Black America has contributed to the condition of Black boys. Now we've gotta turn our tradition of activism inward to inspire our own hearts and then those of our suburban neighbors to act on behalf of our children left in the communities that we seem to have forgotten.

One in a million

I was inspired by Minister Louis Farrakhan's call for atonement 10 years ago. As I shivered my butt off in the brisk October, Washington, D.C. air, I felt that anything was possible. I welled up as I saw men from all over the world embrace and promise each other that we would go home to stand up and be the men that our community needed.

Ten seasons have passed. The air has warmed, then cooled again and still the Black comunity is no better off. HIV/AIDS is now a top killer of Black men between the ages of 25-44 and over half a million of Black men are locked up. This ain't progress. We have not atoned.

In the decade that has passed since the Million Man March I have watched too many bright men and women talk about the problems that we've been having with White people. We sound like abused spouses simultaneously complaining about and justifying our relationship with our abuser. It's time to move on to solutions.

Great minds must settle on devising real solutions. No real solution can begin with, 'If White people would just...' Our issue has never been with all White people.

We can and must save ourselves. I am encouraged to know that the solutions that we seek can be arrived at by regular dudes who have signed up to simply handle their business. There is comfort in knowing that no one expects us to be perfect. They just expect that we, to borrow from Toni Braxton, be a man about it.

Who do you think you are?

Some will question the validity of a perspective on what

Black people should do that is born in a man whose mother is White and father is Black. Since I am such a man, I understand. The history of interracial relations, both among people and within a person, continues to confound and tear at us all. The very question of whom and what is Black has been taken from the trivial to the tragic. Even as I write this I am operating on a definition of Blackness whose roots are in slavery. A reason why I am as aware of issues of race is because I have had to declare mine almost daily.

My racial identity is no question for me though. I do not squirm under questions of 'what are you' or its distant cousin 'where are you from?' White people from my mother to the White parents of a potential prom date have helped me to understand what White is and ain't.

The quest for whom and what is Black can become so muddled that in the end we could feel that either everyone or no one is Black.

Some people count themselves as "all Black." Yet they carry the mark of a European surname and the taint of White ancestors on their skin. Then others are overcome with a need to "acknowledge both sides." So they concoct racial classifications like Tiger Woods' *Cablasian* and Vin Diesel's *Harmony Baby*. I keep it simple. I keep it real. I'm Black. You figure out how.

I know the fluidity and functionality of race in America. I believe that all people want the same thing, to be happy. There is no legitimate physiological or capacity difference between the so-called races. There are however, profound sociological differences, especially for the males.

Being Black and male in America promises a shorter and

less fruitful life. This book is not about the ongoing process of the subjugation of Black people by others. While this is important, we have covered White supremacy for the past generation and look at what that has gotten us.

This book is about what Black people do to further push the poison of racism into our own arms. Then it is about what we need to do to escape our addictions.

Whose side are you on?

Call into question Black people's impact on the condition of Black people and you will be labeled a trader, conservative, Uncle Tom or worse, you will be accused of wanting to be White. Well I don't want to be White, I've had my chance. I want to be part of the solution that begins with being honest with ourselves about what we can do to help ourselves. We can't wait any longer for Jesus, Allah, the government or even the Great Pumpkin to come and save our kids or our community. We need men who know better to man up and do better.

Since nobody is coming to save us I have pointed out pitfalls to progress that stand in the way of Black men taking responsibility for developing solutions for our problems. I have named the names of those who I think have so much more to offer. We cannot afford to lose another generation. Please send help, quick.

Contents

Man up

Mamma's
Boy
Chapter 1

Dear Mamma,

      Get your grown ass son out of your house! Snatch the football comforter off. Grab him by the foot and drag him out of the pee-stained twin bed that he grew up in. Push him past his little league trophies; usher him through the living room where he took prom pictures and throw him out onto the sidewalk that you still have to beg him to shovel when it snows. Close down the kitchen. Stop giving him an allowance. It's time for both of you to move on. There is nothing cool about a man who can't wash his own butt or a mother who keeps him in diapers.

      You are harboring a man who will not take care of his

responsibilities. Stop making excuses for him. He and other unmotivated men like him, are the single, largest problem facing the Black community.

The absence of engaged Black men from the family and community has a more profoundly, negative impact on our children's development than raggedy schools, racism, classism, sexism and joblessness combined. Nobody is in counseling because of racism. Girls don't enter and stay in bad relationships because of the raggedy schools they attended. The lack of self-esteem that stems from not having access to a loving, strong father is literally killing the entire Black community.

Your irresponsible son will worsen the state of Black America. He, plus raggedy schools, racism, classism, sexism and joblessness will equal a bleak future for him, you and us. If we could just get you to make him assume the responsibility of working, going to school and raising children, then you would have done your part.

Women like you are struggling to do it all. Well-meaning women like you are coddling your son, thinking that you are protecting him from the harsh reality of life. You try to do everything for him. When he doesn't deliver, you make excuses or find someone to blame for his shortcomings. He's got you so twisted that you will argue with anybody who dares to hold his feet to the fire of responsibility.

Your unwillingness to let your son learn how to do for himself sets the foundation for a man who cannot and will not ever learn to support himself, his family or add to our community. Your coddling is creating a mutant that wants nothing to do with responsibility.

You still wash your grown son's clothes don't you, don't you? Hell, you probably just got back from New York where you bought him a new wardrobe for his 29th birthday. That's as deep as the white meat. What on earth do you think you are doing?

There's no man who is worth a damn who thinks that it's cool to be taken care of by a woman. Yet you are training him to the contrary? You should be pounding it into his head that a real man should be able to take care of others, not be taken care of by others. You've gotta show him that a real man is an inspired provider.

Only a mamma's boy feels comfortable having a woman take care of him like he is a retarded child. Insects, organisms with brains that could fit on the pointy end of a pin, can take care of themselves. Even bugs find a way to get out of the nest, but mamma's boys spend their entire life under the care of some woman.

We all want you and your son to have a good strong supportive relationship. Our boys need the foundation of the life long maternal bond. Men do marry their mothers. This is why your mother/son relationship is so important. At its best it is a delicate balance of nurturing, which women often excel at, and discipline. So, for example, show him how to iron his pants. Then even if he burns a cavity straight through them, let him learn to do it by himself. It may cost him a pair of pants, but teaching him to do for himself is priceless.

What is at issue is the uneven support that you give that grows into enabling, which leads to teen lethargy and ends up creating a man who never develops beyond being a mamma's boy. You have got to demand that your son learns what it takes to be a man. If that doesn't work, then teach him how you became a strong woman. Anything is better than a mamma's boy.

You know one when you see one

Mamma's boys are lazy and unmotivated, but what makes them most detrimental to the community is that they side-step responsibility. They occupy all professional and socioeconomic sectors. Every family has them. Some families have a few when even one is too many. There are mamma's boys who are doctors, lawyers and Indian chiefs. They are young and as old as a man can get. Their condition is a result of their undirected and uninspired way of life, not what they do for a living.

Mamma's boy are in no rush to take on adult responsibilities like fathering, because they know that their mother lives to give them a way out. Mamma's boys become accustomed to languishing and making the mundane seem impossible as their mother hustles to find excuses, even something to brag about. These guys could provide for themselves but they just won't because they don't have to.

Mamma's boys are looking for low self-esteem, compassion and/or a high threshold for the bull. If you've got any of the aforementioned, then *say hello to your little friend*. He will be a constant point of frustration to you because you know he can do better. Hell he knows that he can do better, but better requires hard work and he's not down with that.

Mamma's boys are raised in one and two parent households. They are in every racial group. The psyche that fosters their development is the same. There is the requisite caregiver, typically a woman or a cast of aunts, grandmothers, cousins, sisters and/or the mother. Then there is a weak or absent father. The woman or women, faced with a weak or absent father, overcompensate for a son who is all too willing to let them. It does take a village to raise a child and any child can become an unproductive mamma's boy when our village combines to limit his access to his responsibility. As long as we let him get away with averting responsibility, he will.

Guilt is the culprit. Somebody is afraid of disciplining the child because they don't want to see him upset. This guilt makes reasonable, loving people say insane things about not wanting to break their son's spirit by telling him no. So they rarely say no. When the adults do say no, it is not final.

The adults are scared to give him structure, simple, loving, necessary structure. Bed times, eating schedules, behavioral expectations, chores, attending school regularly, doing homework, being respectful of authority, you know, basic human stuff is what teaches him how to become a productive citizen. Instead, a mamma's boy is allowed to run amuck. He isn't made to share as a child. Shortly after a minute of 'being good,' there is a shopping spree promised.

The problem is that nobody checks his little butt. When they do, it's too little, too late. He comes to expect that nobody wants to see him upset, so he pouts through life until he gets his way, which mamma usually finds some way to ensure.

A mamma's boy is dangerously charming and pitiful. Never at a loss for words, he can tug on whatever strings you need pulled. Are you impressed by fame? He knows Michael Jordan. His stories are engaging and skillfully dashed with gentle accents of the truth. The issue is not the truth or a lie. Mamma's boys are too skillful for that.

He lurks in the tall grass of nuances. So, yes, he does know

Michael Jordan, just like you know somebody that you met in line at a grocery store. Most people don't expect a person to creep through the muck of nuance, so we see the picture of him and Michael at the grocery store, maybe even him having a phone number and we think, 'he could know him.' Backed by a story or two and we are off telling people that our new friend knows Michael Jordan.

His objective is to be impressive without impressing. A mamma's boy wants to be seen for what he can do without ever having to do anything. His mother never needed him to be anything more than her son, which apparently was impressive to her. She'd dress him up real nice, maybe even put an earring in his five-year-old ear, then she'd put him between her legs to braid his hair and wa la he becomes dote-worthy.

Well here's a hint for you, take that goofy earring out, cut that boy's hair and talk to him about looking and acting like a man. In real life, impressing someone typically takes work. In lieu of work, mamma's boys talk and talk and talk and talk about their potential as their mother's smiling face shines approvingly behind them.

If we believed these men, they are the unluckiest people alive. Their cars break down at an epidemic rate which makes them late or absent from everyhting we need them to do. They have worked for a rash of racist bosses, so many that it seems like the Imperial Grand Wizard of the Ku Klux Klan was their last employer. That's why they can't keep a job. Teachers don't like them. So they failed. Their babies' mothers are all crazy and they get too sick to go to work at a rate of biblical proportions.

Too much time on the nipple leads to chafing

By breast-feeding our young men faulty notions of manhood we are siphoning the life out of the community and ourselves. Accepting his responsibilities will extend the number of years that we will have to work to feed, clothe and house this fraction of a man. Babying a grown ass man emasculates him and decreases the quality of our life.

Every person who deals with one of these spoiled men loses something. The amount that we lose is directly proportionate to the length of time that they are in our lives. He is as useful as a stain on a new dress.

When our sons are shielded from work they never learn to appreciate it or what it can bring. When a mamma's boy sees hard work he is like an infant staring at a life-sized Elmo. He's both fascinated and afraid. He wants to touch the jovial red monster but he's afraid it might hurt him. So he runs and buries his head in his mamma's bosom.

We can no longer burden others with excuses for our son's morbid irresponsibility. His carelessness ensures that we will be grandparents before he is ready to be a father. His acute capriciousness will careen into a young enabling girl just like his enabling caregivers and together they will simultaneously create and ruin another life.

One thing that a mamma's boy has learned is how to get someone else to pick up after him. Right now he's burrowing into the heart of an unsuspecting younger version of us. He's convincing her, just like he does us, that there is no man behind the curtain. She's starting to believe that he is really the Wizard of Oz and, like Dorothy, she will waste her entire life just trying to get back to where she was before she met him.

There's one born every day

Unfortunately, there is always some woman waiting to give up her life to save one of these lost souls. From Compton's streets to college campuses all over this great land of ours, women will defer their dreams to save one of these charismatic bottom feeders. Mamma's boys don't discriminate based upon level of education, income, aesthetics or race. All you've got to do is accept their nonsense and you too can have one of these problems of your very own.

College girls are as susceptible as beauty school dropouts. Money is not a barrier either. Rich girls get taken just like poor ones. Being pretty and thin doesn't make you any less likely to fall prey. Black girls, stop lying to yourselves. White girls don't put up with any more crap than you do. White girls don't buy them any more sneakers than you did nor do they do anything freakier in the bed than he made you, black women, do. The only reason that you know that a White girl is putting up with his foolishness is because you did it first. When he had his fill of you, he left for her. White girls, even the fat ones, are no more likely than you to get '*tooken*' by one of mamma's little wolves.

Once a mamma's boy is embedded in a woman, it could take years to get him out. Restraining orders, angry fathers, hell, not even a sexually transmitted disease will keep him away. He has nothing. He has nothing to lose.

Sister, put your dreams back together

If you want unconditional love, then focus on being lovable. If your father or your son's father left you, then he is a sorry son of a bitch. But absent fathers became irresponsible because there was someone, just like you, who cleaned up their mess. Your son's absent or weak father never had to learn to be responsible because he had you and his parents to take the fall for him.

Your son's father's irresponsibility robbed you of the dreams that you posted on your teenaged walls. Though it is unclear what you lost, it is clear that your relationship with a loser cost you. Now, in addition to the loser that made you mother so tightly, you are creating another loser that you will have to care for long after you are dead.

What are you trying to prove by your unsubstantiated belief in your son? At this point, it is not about your son or his father. It's about you homegirl. It is clear to the rest of us that you need to feel necessary. As long as your son is incapacitated, a social vegetable, you will be needed, so you do nothing that would allow him to become independent, because he will leave you and then what?

For your own sake, you have got to pull up. Get a life. Go back and start to tape together the pieces of your dreams lying on life's floor. Go to school. Get a hobby. Work out. Go to church, mosque, synagogue, and temple. Hit all the bases. Hell, check out Kabala. It worked for Madonna and remember she took naked sex pictures with Vanilla Ice, Big Daddy Kane and a dog. Things have got to be better for you.

Your son's father's selfishness snatched down your dreams then ripped them to shreds. While your beautiful little boy cried in the background, you were left to spend the rest of your life salvaging the remnants of what you thought you would become. You may have wanted to be a lawyer, now you simply find yourself arguing a lot. You may even be a lawyer who wanted a supportive husband, but your last date was with your son at Chuck E. Cheese. What you dreamed of having in your adult life has been pawned so that you could become two parents. Now your son is your world and the little boy knows it. Love him. And love you. Both are necessary.

You were enamored with his father, but now you are dating his son. That's pretty creepy when you think about. This is the reverse of the whole Freudian Oedipus complex that typically occurs when the child is in love with the parent of the opposite sex. Ew…

You have developed an unhealthy infatuation for your son that you use to prop you up while it tears him down. Mary Kay Letourneau went to jail for something like that. Remember her? She's the former California teacher who fell in love with, had two kids with and left her husband for a middle school student? She couldn't separate adult to child love either nor did she understand boundaries. Good touch and bad touch are one in the same in her strange world. Now we know that she's crazy. So what's your deal?

Stop dating your kid. He's cute, but he's not that damn cute. Get him out of your bed. Don't lie to him and tell him that he's the man of the house. Don't consult him about men that you're interested in and don't let him think that he has a say in how you spend your time. You are the parent and he is the kid. (Say that 100 times in your head.) He is developing a bloated sense of self. This is never a good thing.

Parenting alone is the hardest thing anyone can do

Raising a kid alone, even if you are married, has got to be the hardest thing to do on earth. This is why the rest of us need to be there for you, supporting you and at times reminding you of what you went through so that your son doesn't grow up to treat another woman the same way you were treated by his father.

We can't let you forget how you felt having to take care of him by yourself. We must encourage you to think of how you felt taking care of a boy who longed for two responsible parents.

You must always remember the struggles of parneting alone. You know what it is like when his father didn't play a role. We need you to reflect on the emotions that meander from wanting to kill him to wanting help so badly that you agree to put up with your son's father's foolishness.

Recount the times that you lied to your baby boy about why his father didn't come through with the winter coat that he promised. Then take yourself back to how you felt when you were pleading with his father to just go to one doctor's appointment because you couldn't get out of work. There is no way that you can forget the nights that you cried yourself to sleep as your sick son screamed beside you in your bed with a 101-degree temperature. Can you remember what it would have meant to have had help when you were tired? Didn't you long for someone else to give him a bath some nights, check his homework some nights and answer his endless questions every day?

Imagine passing this life on to another woman. She's young and pretty, like you were. She's got a big heart, big dreams and low self-esteem, just like you have. She's got her wedding day planned, including colors and bridesmaids' gowns, the same as you. She has an office with degrees on the walls in her future too. She has envisioned those same cars, clothes and vacations that made you go out on that cold dark morning to wait for the school bus when you were her age.

She too dreams that the winds of love will rush through and kick up a field of butterflies within her. She wants a husband and family just like you. No, she's not your daughter, but she is your sister. Now ask yourself, can I trust my son with her, I mean your..., I mean her dreams?

The unspeakable, ugly truth

The Black nuclear family has been decimated. Cities and suburbs are filled with Black mothers and Black children, each having different last names. Where are the fathers? Only God knows.

Single parenthood limits our children's emotional development, daily academic preparation and long-term quality of life. By extension, neighborhoods of single mothers are significant reasons why our children and schools are failing. When anyone has too many kids to monitor, child and community lose. One child can be, and too often is, too much for a single mom to bring up by herself.

There is not a single indicator of quality of life that is higher for children attached to only parent versus that of children raised by both parents; even if the parents are not together. Not one. Not school performance, health or income. Nothing. According to the US Census, the poorest people in the United States are the children of single women. The second poorest are the women themselves. Kids with both parents in their life simply live happier healthier lives.

We've got too many Black kids coming into large urban schools from homes that can't support their need to perform well in school. Success in school is directly linked to quality of life. Conversely failure in school is for many, a precursor to a difficult life. Simply put, women cannot raise our kids by themselves.

It is a big lie that a woman can work and raise kids alone. Has it happened? Yes. Every single day there are examples of extraordinary women, kids and their support networks that combine to do amazing things. My mother is just such a woman. She had me on her sixteenth birthday. Now, because her drive and the tremendous support of my grandmother and aunts, she and I both have college degrees. However, there is no denying the failure rates for children coming from single parent households. So anecdotes of the superwomen give us no insight into the harsh truth.

Decreased time on the task of nurturing her children decreases the probability that single mothers will be able to make sure that their kids' homework is done, for instance. This should not be seen as an excuse for single moms to avoid going to games and meetings with teachers. Nor is it a *fait accompli* for their kids. The human spirit is at times indelible. It is however, a very real reason why so many of our schools suck and our communities are dangerous and undesirable.

Single working women are not the villains though. The limits of their resources are. The reason that their resources are limited is because they created a child with a loser. Deadbeat fathers leave our women and children to fend for themselves. They provide no regular support or direction. Communities with the highest incidence of the deadbeat fathers are the most susceptible to becoming a *Lord of the Flies* child headed island where kids make adult decisions

23

and fail.

The problem of single parenthood then is with men who do not take care of their children. Leaving a woman to do what takes both a man and woman is why we are not able to give our kids the support that they need. It is simply amazing that so many women are able to accomplish what they do on their own. It is equally amazing that a man who is not taking care of his kids can sleep at night. There is a special place in hell for a man who leaves his children.

It makes me sick to hear men complaining about how they can't see their kids. Please. Tell somebody who doesn't really know that there is a child and woman who would probably give an arm for him to bring his ass over just once a month. Are some women tough to deal with? Of course, but the majority need a hand so they'll learn to chill to get some help. The bottom line is that men who want to be in their kids' lives are. Those who don't have a heap of excuses and someone to support them.

Raise a son who you would want to marry, don't marry your son

Raise a man who you would want your daughter to marry. One who can and will take care of himself and his family. This is a goal of parenting. Good people are not defined by degrees, clothing or who they know. They are measured on characteristics like living to improve the lives of others.

Your tolerance for a mamma's boy is clear. You laid with one. Now you're raising one. To make up for his father's shortcomings you have given what feels like everything and your son, like the parasite that he is, will leave you empty.

Sacrifice is something you know all too well, yet you keep

this lesson locked away from your son like detergent. Instead you teach him that buying him $120 sneakers every six months shows him love. That's part of the problem. Love is love. There is no substitute. Teaching your son the value of money and work, for instance, by making him work to buy his own $50 sneakers and then putting the remaining $70 dollars into a college fund, now that's love. That's a deep and abiding love that says that I love you so much that I am going to teach you words like sacrifice, investment and modesty in preparation for your future as a father, husband and reliable member of the community.

The size of your heart made you this way. Really. You are among those very special people who can love beyond reason into the ridiculous. You see hope where the rest of us see hopelessness. Through your eyes your boy always deserves one more chance. You see what he could be. You believe in the unbelievable. Your blind faith has led you into the cult of women who love through the bars of men's stupid decisions.

On some level you are to be commended, admired even. You have seen light in the pitch of darkness. You saw his talent and you believed him when he said that he was 'bout to take out the trash; 'bout to clean his room; 'bout to do well in school; 'bout to go to college; 'bout to get a job; 'bout to get a record deal; 'bout to start going to church, and 'bout to make you proud. Unfortunately, when the lights come on, like anybody else who takes it too far, you end up with a mouth full of it, looking silly, really, really silly.

The bitter medicine of failure is the mamma's boy antidote

If you're feeling the urge to try to correct your little life long burden and you want to point him toward the road of self-sufficiency, then try teaching him words like 'please' and 'thank you'. It's a great place to start. Teach him simple, clear and consistent structure, the type that effectively teaches responsibility. Then show him how responsiveness to the needs of others is at the center of every successful relationship.

When the soft approach doesn't work, then get medieval on his butt. Give him ultimatums. Tell him to get a job, start doing well in school, take care of his responsibilities or he's got to get out of your life. You wouldn't invite a stranger into your life who brought almost nothing to the table, so why are you allowing him to live off of you for free? Is it because you're afraid that your son will fail? You know him well. Failure is a great teacher.

You say that you know that he is not an angel, so why do you treat him like he is one? When he does something stupid, discipline, even if it comes too swift or harsh. Stop fussing with teachers, girlfriends, family and friends.

Let him learn how to fight and lose his own battles. This is what a responsible man does. When a real man starts some mess he is ready to finish it. He doesn't need his mother to loan him money to pay his cell phone bill. Are you kidding me? What kind of grown man borrows money from his mother? When you let him learn how to handle his business, he will not start a fight that he can't finish because he knows what it will cost.

Give him a chance to taste the bitter medicine of failure. Don't wait for somebody who doesn't care about him to take things he cares about away, simulate it. Failure, even practiced, will cure his expectation that somebody will always take care of him.

Let him do it wrong and deal with the consequences all by himself. You don't have to raise Winston Churchill. All we are

asking for is a regular kid who tries and fails, then tries again. The
hallmark of a winner is that he always has one more try in him.

We have to prepare our kids

The primary responsibility of raising and educating Black
kids sits squarely in the laps of Black families. All families have to
send kids into the world prepared to learn otherwise, junk in junk
out.

The process of obtaining a formal education is a metaphor. It
no longer represents learning about slope, base and height.
Succeeding in school is the process of learning how to deal with
what life lays before our sons.

Preparation has to start when our boys are young. When a
parent sends a kid to school unprepared everybody loses. It is hard
for even a good teacher to teach children who aren't prepared to
learn. Good schools formulate curriculum on the presumption that
the children can be successful in the classroom. The curriculum also
presumes that the lessons will be expounded on at home.

If the process of going to school is a life metaphor, then by
extension, our schools can be seen as a representation of our
community. When kids enter our schools or community unprepared
and unrehearsed, it hurts the other kids in the community too.
Teachers, employers and friends are forced to stop or slow down in
order to accommodate the unprepared kids. Of course the child
who came to the community unprepared loses the most. As the
prepared kids wait, they learn nothing and we as a community are
stagnant.

Only we can prevent mamma's boys

Family and friends, we are charged with stopping the spread of the mamma's boys. Their dependency hurts our community. There is no such position as spectator when it comes to mamma's boys. They have been programmed to do as little as possible. They have a sick dependency on their first crush, their mother.

Whatever our relation to mamma's boy are, we can be sure of two things; they will have good stories and poor follow through. We are all bridges over their responsibility. They have no problem letting us pay their way, in fact they prefer it because it reminds them of life with mom. Hard work is for suckers like us, and their mothers. We owe it to these brothas to correct them before they 'borrow' again.

Black communities have no more vacancies for useless men. Generations of them are still living amongst us. They are killing our community from the inside as we speak. In our collective efforts to right mamma's boys' wrongs, we spill into the streets to demonstrate, are forced into courtrooms, and fill the pages of the academy with excuse after excuse as to why they still need our nurturing support for their foolishness. We have spent too much time explaining this nonsense. Damn the system. This is some regular ol' laziness that has got to stop. Tell them to get a job, move out and move on. They are an embarrassment.

We are paying dearly for those who are not pulling their weight. Our community needs all of our men. We need them to teach, coach, counsel, create businesses, write books, raise families, and to just be decent human beings. The Black community just needs regular dudes. We need them to be able to give love, be compassionate partners, useful friends and good neighbors.

The Black community needs regular men to help us move our sister into their new apartment, on the fifth floor, with no elevator in August, because that's what real men do. We need them to tell us what's wrong with our car and what is right about our dreams. We need them to lead. We need them to follow. We can't send another Black man to jail. We need their beauty and the bending tides of their imperfection. We need our boys to grow up to be good average men who add more than they take, love more than they hate and heal more than they hurt.

Mammas don't let your babies grow up to be sorry

While our community does not have a patent on the bloodsucking design, we might have perfected it. If we never raise another mamma's boy it would be too soon. How do you know if your son, boyfriend, husband, nephew, brother, cousin, student or grandson is a mamma's boy? Consider the following questions and statements. Score on a scale of zero to five. Five is the truest statement and zero means that it is false. The lower the score the better the man. Get it? Okay, see you after the quiz!

Is he a mamma's boy?

Disagree	0
Barely	1
Sometimes	2
Yes	3
Definitely	4
All of the time	5

1. He takes pride in having someone else take care of his responsibilities.
2. He receives regular financial support from someone else.
3. More than once since he's been an adult, he has lived somewhere that he has not paid for. This includes staying with his mother, girlfriend or at one of his boys' houses.
4. He is one of the last people that you think of when you need help.
5. He puts himself and his interests before everyone elses.
6. When you communicate with him it's not uncommon for the conversation to entail addressing his mounting needs.
7. Others generosity is essential to his survival.
8. His big plans and short follow through yields little more than near misses and compelling stories about brushes with fame and fortune.
9. It takes him twice as long and thrice as much prodding to get him to finish tasks, ranging from helping around the house, to getting a job, to paying his bills, to completing his education.
10. You have stopped depending on him and now presume that it is not even worth asking him for help.

What this unscientific quiz means

Scores of 1-6

You've got an earner. Find a way to keep him in your life. Even if he's a friend, he will contribute more than he takes. He's reliable and could easily be a role model to both men and women. His work ethic is impeccable and he is dependable.

Scores of 7-17

He is still an asset. If this were a credit rating, he'd still be worth the risk. He's got more up than down. He's still overwhelmingly dependable and capable of enriching your life. He'll be there for you when you need him and he recognizes that the world does not revolve around him.

Scores of 18-28

Well, things are starting to turn. He likes to have his fun, not too much, but enough to cause quite a few arguments with someone who depends on him to start a future. He goes to work and maybe even has a career, but his priorities are blurry. His friends and his own interests are important. Settling down is not a priority now. He's not nesting. He's floating around enjoying the scenery. He has a high upside and visible faults. He is lovable and charming, a lot of fun and a lot of work.

Scores of 29-39

What have you gotten yourself into? Whether he's your friend, family or partner, your relationship with him has already cost you. His debts have become yours. His excuses leave gaps that you will need to fill. He is not a worker. He is not focused. He is driven by self-interest and is therefore skillfully manipulative. He's burned bridges and dear friends. He has spent quite a few nights on somebody's couch, in their basement or guest room because he was supposed to have done something but, 'see what had happened was….' Cut your losses and allow him to fall the rest of the way by himself or be prepared to go down with him. He wants only what he can take and, as sweet as he may be, he is a danger to himself and others. He has nothing to contribute beyond empty promises and whatever he has borrowed. He's a whirlwind of potential and potential doesn't fill the belly. Leave him alone.

Scores of 40-50

You listened to none of your friends. Even admitting certain things for this quiz was a chore. He's got you and man does it hurt. None of us can understand what on earth you are doing. We want to feel sympathy for you, but to date you have shunned every ounce of help that has been offered to you. We think you like it. We think that you enjoy having him around, no matter what the cost. Your credit, your friends and your sanity are his to devour. You have spent more time compensating for his shortcomings than addressing your own. You are as hopeless as a penny with a hole in it. All we can do is watch as you twist in the wind. You got yourself tangled up in this mess and, as much as we want to, we can't do a damn thing to help. There is little use in telling you about him because his actions are so blatant that talking about him would be like describing the night. It is what it is. This relationship is all about you. It was you who brought him into your life and it will be you who takes him out or it will be you who invites him to take you out. Good luck and Godspeed.

Thugs and Other Stupid Mess Chapter 2

The Black community builds thugs

Thugs are screw-faced, intellectually, pubescent boys parading through our neighborhoods like ants dutifully marching to the military cadence of urban drums. They are do-ragged pant-saggers climbing in and out of our windows, making themselves at home on our couches, televisions and in our fiction. Thugs are the measure of a man for many people. They are rough necked and dangerous, willing to pop a gat in you while getting lifted on chronic. Emotionless, thugs reproduce seeds like an oak in fall, littering our cities and towns and overcrowding our schools. Revered and feared, reviled and sought after, pitied and praised, they are our sons, brothers, nephews and cousins. They are the epitome of life and personification of death. Thugs. Is this the best we have to offer?

From the earliest of experiences, these bad boys have a way of getting all the attention. Families bend in the direction of the troubled youth, pushing aside the bland taste of good grades and satisfactory behavior for the intoxication of the little boy who can't seem to stay out of trouble.

The Black community builds thugs. We foster their development when we apologize for, instead of correcting the havoc that they create. We teach thugs to be who they become and then blame the world for the negativity that they bring.

The biography of a thug

Thugs start as misguided kids who have not been taught to positively express some of the most basic human characteristics like compassion, discomfort and confusion. These scared maladjusted young men are not tough.

Preachers who challenge the government, they're tough. Trash collectors who rise before dawn to feed their families, these cats are tough. Lawyers and businessmen who forgo the quest for cash in exchange for community renewal, now they are tough. But little boys who threaten the sanctity of innocent decent people are some of the softest people you will ever come across. Sure they'll get into a physical fight, but not without a crew or a weapon. What's tough about that? All thugs are scared little boys who need some direction and a hug.

Their negative actions should not be confused with deeds of honor and valor. They are not freedom fighters getting locked up for 25 years like Nelson Mandela. They rob and terrorize us. This is not cool. They are common urchins who want nothing more than to take what is not theirs. They want to piss on the efforts of those who have died so that we may be seen as humans. Their bizarre commitment to maintaining a dangerous exterior has no community value. None. Black thugs make being Black a freaking liability.

Thugs are absolutely petrified of being labeled soft. A thug is so scared of looking soft that he won't even wear eyeglasses because of the stigma attached. Now a thug will don sunglasses though, even inside a dark club at night, because he thinks that this will make him look tough. No he won't be able to see a thing, but he looks tough, dark and mysterious. Ooh that's so sexy…. You might think that a thug isn't dancing because he doesn't like to. The truth is he probably can't find the dance floor. By the middle of the night he has bumped into so many things that sitting down is the best he can do until the lights come back on.

By the 7th grade it becomes painfully clear that some of our boys ain't gonna make it. A dull glaze covers their eyes. Their tendency to consistently do dumb things is so inculcated that there is little hope for them. They are beaten. These kids are caught up in the undertow of a system that they did not create but that has positioned them for self-destruction.

They have lost hope for a future so they live life in pieces. Today is the alpha and omega of their life. Broken homes and promises lead them into the streets. Raggedy schools, inconsistent role models and ineffective discipline set the direction into the bleak ally of thug life. Thugs have not learned to connect their actions to reactions. Cause and effect are peculiar if not esoteric concepts that hang in the distance like a dimming star.

Who becomes a thug

Two types of boys become thugs that are followers and quitters. Both groups of boys feel uncomfortable in their own skin. They both so badly need to be validated that they're willing to affiliate with the most ridiculous mess.

The first group reads and computes slower than the other kids. Instead of accepting the challenges of their undeserved shortcomings, they act like idiots. Thugs are identified and identify themselves as being bad kids. There has always been someone in their life willing to support the concept that they're bad. So when their caregiver was asked, 'How's your son?' they'd answer proudly, 'Bad as hell.' This set the stage and the little boy has just been acting the part ever since. These slower boys call upon the perception of being bad when trying becomes too hard and acting like a fool too easy.

The second group of boys that are set up to become thugs can read and compute very well, but, because it ain't cool to be smart, they too act like fools. Not doing any of their homework and still pulling C's is the hallmark of a smart kids who want to fit in with the negative element. Our smart thugs in waiting do stupid mess like stealing an earring, even though it's fake gold and they have the money to pay for it. Remember, these boys know better, but being bad is so much cooler than being good. God has a strange way of dispensing talent to those who seem to appreciate it the least.

Thugs are followers. Sure, they'll lead other followers, but they are too scared to be courageous enough to go it alone. Both have turned off their good sense in exchange for acceptance. The only people who will accept their constant stupidity are people who live to do stupid mess, thugs.

Everybody wants to be a thug

When a White person says Black people are stupid, this is racist. When a Black kid commits to personifying ignorance, this too is racist and more damaging. Racist words can disappear into the air in which they were spoken. Internalized racist actions leave marks that stain the actor and audience.

Too many of our college boys believe that Black and ignorant are synonymous. Now thousands of them pander to this ridiculousness, throwing away the hard-fought victories that put them on that campus.

Our community is in crisis and thugs are a reason. They have connived their way into our hearts. There is no more powerful example of the impact of the thug mentality on our community than in our talented tenth. Once the hope of a race, now gifted Black boys can be found walking around college campuses with their pants hanging off their butts, blaring music in their huge headphones on their way past the library to a dorm where they will play video games all afternoon. From the Ivy League to a local community college, gifted Black boys think that the only way for them to be seen as Black is for them to wear the costume, assume the language and engage in the habits of thugs.

Bright Black kid after bright Black kid leaves home for college to dummy down their language and abandon the work ethic that got them there. Even with the world on a string, smart Black boys who've never been in a fight go to college and become hard-core.

Newsflash, thugs don't take the SAT or ACT, they don't

enroll in college prep classes and they don't do homework. They are thugs for God's sake. Yet college-bound kids do. Thugs' high school behavior prepares them for prison. College-bound kids' high school behavior prepares them for college. It is, therefore, unconscionable that a child would avoid thug behavior for 17 years in preparation for college, get to campus and regress beyond anything that even they have ever done.

The impact of thugs on the Black community

Let one White police officer kill one Black boy who was out running the streets at 2:00 AM on a Tuesday and Black people will march, call for reforms, scream racism and spray murals of the slain child on other people's property. But when we kill our own every single day where's the outcry? Sure, we pour out a little liquor, get some iron-on letters to make a R.I.P. t-shirt, then we start back down the road of blaming the White man for bringing weapons and crack into the Black community. What if we began to attack the racist lethal behavior of our boys with the same vigor that we do the racist lethal behavior of cops?

There is no rash of White marauders haunting the streets of Houston, Harlem, Hartford, Philly or Compton murdering thousands of Black people a day. It's our boys. Every single day, hour after horrifying hour, Black boy after Black boy is being killed by friendly fire and we silently understand.

We are losing the battle for control of our future in our streets. Our communities are war zones because we are allowing the scourge that has infested it to kill potential at its root. What if cancer had a cure but its 16-year-old Black male founder lie in a box awaiting burial after being shot by another 16-year-old Black male?

Only God knows. What if Muhammad Ali wasn't the greatest? What if he was just one of ten, but the other nine split their deaths between prison and the innocence of association with that era's version of thugs. What if we had given birth to ten of the first Black presidents and just as quickly killed them off? What if one of the ten did make it but he was too ashamed to study hard for fear that he'd be picked on? What if Einstein was a hack compared to the little Black boy who got caught selling crack for the third time? Now he is underemployed and his methods to convert the sun into a usable form of energy are tucked deep behind his undeveloped potential. The same communities and struggles that create the culture and supports the development of the thug mentality also give rise to greatness. Many a world leader has risen from their nation's slums to inspire us all. This litany of hope lost is brought to you in part by your local thugs.

We cannot depend on schools, public or private, to fix our thugged out boys. The government? Please. We have seen these institutions enslave, undereducate and then imprison our boys. Only a fool would depend upon them to solve problems that start in our homes.

It all starts with us

When purely negative behaviors are not squashed, even good kids begin to feel like being tough is not enough. They have to become a thug to be safe. So look into the eyes of our thug heroes. Smell the death that they peddle. See the schools that they ruin. Then you will understand how the National Center for Educational Statistics has found that 74% of schools with at least 50% minority children are violent, (1999-2000, NCES, Table 7.1). This same

39

report states that our kids, more than any other, experienced crimes like rape, sexual battery other than rape, physical attack or fights with a weapons, threats of physical attack with weapons, and robbery with or without weapons in their schools, (1999-2000, NCES, Table 7.1).

Thugs make our schools dangerous for teachers too. From 1998-2002, 141,600 urban teachers were victimized in their own schools according to the NCES. Nearly half of the urban teachers who were victims of crime, 68,000, experienced violent or serious crimes ranging from rape to robbery with or without a weapon, (1998-2002, NCES, Table 9.1). That's right, teachers being raped on the job in our schools.

Watch as thugs rip apart families by robbing us of the potential that is bubbling in the lives they have taken. Indulge in the stench of fear that lingers in our air. These cute and cuddly thugs that MC Lyte and Destiny's Child sing about so lovingly are the ones who most terrorize our communities. Our Black sons have us more afraid of ourselves than we have ever been of White folks or Islamic Fundamentalists.

Imagine, if you will, if every Black person who lived with other Black people felt safe. Imagine looking into the night and realizing that there is a group of five Black boys walking behind you and making you feel safe. Picture our corners and community colleges clear of intimidating groups of rude kids, our secondary schools filled with respectful young men and our families without the burden of another visit to a local jail. Imagine Black communities in which Black people formed a moratorium on Black on Black crime. Now open your eyes. What do you see?

Apologists and posers

Public discourse is crowded with apologists and posers, from the left and the right, who are mishandling the opportunity to correct the purely negative impact that the thug culture is having on the Black community.

The apologists bore us with refried blaming expeditions in which the White man is the desired prey. The posers plant the poles that are sticking out of their butts on a church lawn calling their cause one of decency. Both groups are equally off base and ineffective. They succeed only in leaving thugs and their destructive habits in place to eat away at the Black community.

The glow of thugs' charisma even fools the great minds of our time. The genius Reverend Dr. Michael Eric Dyson, professor of humanities and African-American studies at the University of Pennsylvania, has committed pounds of his precious intellect to an ongoing idolatry of thugs. Indeed, Dr. Dyson has and will do more great things for Black people than most. Sadly though, Dr. Dyson has spent more time in recent years trying to publicly explain the inexplicable, far-reaching impact of real thugs and their entertainer alter egos - rappers. He's touring the country sweating kids like 50 Cent and the Ying Yang Twins. The professor's meal ticket though is the slain entertainer and self-proclaimed 'Thug for life,' Tupac Shakur.

Gangster rappers are proud thugs. They entrance us with story after story of how they are former drug dealing misogynistic thugs. They are so deft in their rhymes about undermining our community that we drink it like Jim Jones' red Kool Aide. Instead of having the will to correct these brothas, apologists like Dr. Dyson are whining and making excuses. Every single time apologists romanticize the mayhem that the thug lifestyle wreaks on every single Black man, woman and child or softens thugs' message, an opportunity is lost to save that thug and our community from its most prolific enemy - itself.

Dr. Dyson represents herds of apologists who accept no responsibility for the Black condition. These hapless do-gooders have got a systemic excuse for every single bad habit these kids have. Apologists spend countless hours putting us to sleep with thin explanations for the perpetuation of the thug culture.

Dr. Dyson, the quintessential thug sympathizer, has taken to burning Tupac's verses into his ample vocabulary in an apparent attempt to connect with a generation that had more interest in him when he wasn't a rap impresario.

Imagine Malcolm X wasting his time memorizing and then reciting Snoop Dog's lyrics in an effort to connect to young people. Even Snoop's chronically altered mind has trouble wrapping itself around that one. We cannot continue to turn a blind eye to the behavior of those who tear apart our community. We are out of eyes.

The disorder that thugs call for cannot be combated by immersion in their lyrical chaos. Thousands of activists, both Black and White did not suffer horrible pain and humiliation for today's adults to start following and quoting misguided kids. The giants of the civil rights era knew that in order to save our community we needed to challenge the entire community to ascend to the highest values of selflessness, compassion, discipline and order. Rosa Parks didn't sit for this so we can't stand for it. To save our community we must claim a jihad on all who attack her, whether they look like us or not.

Celebrating the entertainment value of thugs is analogous to explaining the cultural relevance of Aunt Jemima. It makes some sense that Tupac, a kid killed at 25, spent so much time idolizing thugs. It makes no sense that a Princeton University educated Ph.D. and Christian minister like Dr. Dyson spends so much time sweating all things 'Pac. Tupac didn't think about Tupac as much as Dr. Dyson does. Dr. Dyson's profound intellectual sophistication somehow has gotten twisted and now dangles like a microphone cord from 'Pac's nuts.

In a 2001 interview published in his book *Open Mic*, Dr. Dyson compares Tupac with St. Paul, (you know, the one from Corinthians who brought us scriptural hits like 'When I was a child I spoke as a child…'); Freidrich Nietzsche and L. A. Feuerbach, (I had to Google both of them to find out that they were 19th Century religious critics); B.B. King and Mahalia Jackson, (legends of Blues and Gospel, respectively); Dr. Martin Luther King, Jr., (Nobel Prize winning civil rights pioneer and martyr); as well as Langston Hughes, and Zora Neal Hurston, (authors of cannons of African American literature too vast and compelling to abbreviate).

Well damn. Dr. Dyson's characterization seems a bit lofty for Tupac Shakur, the author of, "F**k you losers, while you fake jacks I make maneuvers. Like Hitler stickin' up Jews wit German lugers, (Tupac Shakur, *All Eyez on Me*, Got my Mind Made Up)."

Read many gangster rappers' lyrics without the mastery of legendary rap producers like Dr. Dre and their songs are boring diatribe shortcuts to a premature exit, not a topic worthy of pondering. These kids' songs and the thug behavior that they claim to depict sound more like a cross between a ransom and a suicide note written by somebody with a third-grade education.

Tupac Shakur and the Notorious B.I.G. remain publicly traded representations of a problem that has seeped into the pores of our community. The problem is with the Black community's eternal fear of public correction.

Apologists want us to believe that if we correct our kids publicly we are traitors. It is disappointing that Dr. Dyson, a scholar who has written definitive works on men such as Dr. King and Malcolm X, has traded in his good sense for a career of protecting the guilty. As if this were not bad enough, now he is branching off into the absurd world of prosecuting the innocent.

In Dr. Dyson's bizarre fanaticism to sell books, he said that Dr. Bill Cosby is a villain and pornography-peddling pubescents are heroes. Dr. Dyson treats Dr. Bill Cosby, a man who has lost his own son to gun violence, and continuing to send thousands of Black boys and girls to college, like a traitor. Dr. Dyson should be ashamed. Dr. Cosby should be proud.

Most of us don't have the luxury of pontificating about the fate of the Black community from an Ivy League skybox. From up there, where most of the students are White or Asian and extremely wealthy, the struggle looks different. The rest of us see what happens when we praise negativity. Kids get hurt. Our community crumbles. Our future dims.

When you are on the dirt floor of the coliseum with the lions, there is no time to turn away the support of the likes of Dr. Cosby for the promised doom that thugs bring. Visiting college campuses for $10,000 per hour can create a cognitive dissonance, which could lead to cultural dementia. This is a condition in which the enemy becomes the hero. From Dr. Dyson's lofty perch, it does not matter what happens to the community that you misrepresent, you're still getting paid.

None of us wants to give up on our kids, so when they are doing anything but selling drugs, intimidating people or otherwise being useless, we tend to get excited. If they are rapping we think, at least they're not selling drugs. What a low threshold for our community to set for its children. At least they're not selling drugs?

Flailing in the mire of abject negativity, our boys are digging a hole and covering themselves with what will be the dirt of our destruction. No one rises to low expectations. We have come to accept the worst that our boys have to offer and they are giving it to us tenfold in every expression of them, which includes their music.

Posers, like the overzealous, shortsighted civil rights activists, the late C. Delores Tucker and Reverend Calvin Butts will not solve the thug problem either. Neither will right-winged publicity sluts like Bill O'Reilly. They, too, are overwhelmed by the same insincere, selfish hunt for glory that inspired the thugs. Buying and crushing CD's like Tucker and Butts did in the mid-90's was a flat and unimpressive publicity stunt that a decade later hasn't shown a single sign of improving anything more than their visibility.

Now even Bill O'Reilly, a former gossip show talking head, can euphemistically hop on the pig pile that is the anti-Hip Hop culture effort. He can join the legions that connect Hip Hop and Black people to the undermining of the 'American way.' To men like O'Reilly all of Hip Hop is negative because it's not Rock n' Roll. Now *Bill O'Reilly* cares about the portrayal of the Black community? Riiiight. Since when? He, like all the rest of the posers, are not going to solve the problems depicted in the music or communities it represents. All they are going to do is make a lot of dollars and no change. Too many kids will still be thugs and the

Black community will still be their primary victims.

Nothing that these folks have done has helped our kids or the communities they are destroying. Apologists think that if we just understand what our boys are going through, then find a systemic culprit, the problem will solve itself. The culpability of our boys does not exist in their worldview. To them, our boys are simply victims incapable of lifting the rock of 400 years of racism.

These posers' self-aggrandizements are the other side of a missed opportunity to change the hearts of the thug element of the community. They feel that if the kids would just buy new clothes, talk proper English, stop listening to Hip Hop and go to church, the problem would take care of itself. The system's negative impact has passed because if one can make it, then everybody can. For them, personal responsibility itself is what is at the core of our demise.

The truth is that we have all combined to create a horrible condition in our community. Both apologists and posers have had their chance to deal with this and all that has happened is that it has gotten worse. Now it is time for the progressives to flush out the foolishness wherever it resides, including the systems and individuals, both internal and external. We understand that sometimes we are to blame while at other times the problem lies somewhere else. Progressives know that the source of our downward spiral is not a static target. We know that the barriers to progress move from one part of the community to the other, from person to person, inside out. Until we stop blaming and start addressing the morphing dilemmas affecting the Black community, it will continue to overtake us.

The chickens have come home to roost

When we do not attempt to correct negative behavior we become its victims. Hip Hop is more than the music of our community. It is a community in itself. Its established habits and language is as significant as those of the baby boomers. Therefore, the music must more accurately reflect the best that we have to offer. Hip Hop's artists, topics and consumers range from our children to our young professionals. We cannot continue to represent them as being pumped full of junk.

When Hip Hop became Gangster Rap and started mistreating the community, its perpetrators should have been corrected, swiftly and completely. Rappers like Chuck D should have turned the SW1's loose on the affected thugs. KRS One knew better than to let them bastardize the hard-fought battles for rap supremacy with violent street brawls. He too said nothing against those who'd arrested control of the art form. Russell Simmons knows better too. His Hip Hop threw parties and steadied a late 80's movement for intellectual enlightenment. These men combined to exemplify Hip Hop as well as our young men's direction and purpose. Unfortunately, as Gangster Rap arrived, battle tested lyrical warriors stood by as new jack hoodlums snatched their chains. The complexity of loving the community enough to both understand personally and correct publicly was too much. They did not want to roll on a brotha' so they let Hip Hop be dragged all the way to Death Row.

We must refuse to let Trick Daddy and Murder Inc. wrestle from us what's left of Hip Hop or the community it represents. We're not ready for a blanket in the park at the summer jazz series. We're not feeling finger snapping poetry slams with fat women complaining about not finding love. It was fun being Naughty by Nature. We still thrive on the base of our youth and the groove of Common. It is Mos' definitely time for the Dead Prez to rise. The Hip Hop community's vast, yet misguided talent, needs to be brought back and made positive again.

The self-destructive tendencies displayed in the Black community through our habits are mirrored via ghastly images portrayed in Hip Hop culture. The negative impact of embracing negative imagery does not affect the Black and White communities equally. When the White rapper Eminem rhymes about destroying his rivals with the same venom, vigor and methods so aptly used by his Black predecessors, he wins an Oscar.

White people are not seen as being more dangerous because Eminem raps about brutally killing his ex-wife and the mother of his daughter. Eminem is instead traded to the Black community in a Dave Chappelle-inspired racial draft where the White people take Colin Powell and Condoleezza Rice and we are left with yet another foul-mouthed, albeit terribly talented, little boy.

What Eminem says makes him seem real. When Beanie Sigel does it, we are threats to the wellbeing of humanity. When gay rights groups picket Eminem there are no undertones of racism, it's about him, his words, his deeds, and his music, not White people. The 'Eminem Factor' points to the disparity between the impacts of publicly spun negative imagery, as seen in Gangster Rap. Black people cannot push negativity without it lessoning our stake in the American Dream. Is it hypocritical for Wal-Mart to sell guns, but refuse to sell CD's with the word gun spoken? Hell yes. But we are not going to transform our community or remove the majority of community's hypocrisy by playing to the fears that fuel it.

When President John F. Kennedy was killed by an assassin's bullet, Malcolm X reacted. He said that when you covet violence it will come back to claim you. He said that the President's actions leading up to his death had allowed violence to fester in the country and it, like the chickens at the end of the day, had returned home to roost.

Tupac and Biggie signed a blood pact that cost them their lives. They, like too many of our boys, did end up "representin'." They represented what happens when the Hip Hop community does all that we can to portray ourselves as violent-minded animals that seek to maim and kill. Now, like so many of our men, both rappers are young and dead.

It is fitting that Biggie was murdered following a *Vibe Magazine* party. This magazine's editors and writers virtually created the East Coast/West Coast feud that many believe claimed the lives of both Biggie and Tupac. *Vibe* and *Source* magazines devoted cover after cover to what was simply an issue between two young boys. These magazines are self-proclaimed protectors of Hip Hop, yet they sold us and these two boys out by passing pungent images off as entertainment. The writers and editors responsible for the ongoing exploitation of Tupac and Biggie are nothing more than pencil pushing hustlers who are short on original ideas and long on their commitment to selling magazines at all costs. They need to give these boys' images back to their families and find something else to write about.

The *Source* and *Vibe*, along with other lesser-known Hip Hop magazines' critical analysis of 'Pac and Biggie has been served on a postpartum plate. Now they get their quarterly Biggie and Tupac fix through anniversary issues, unsolved mystery issues, the greatest rappers of all time issues and the ubiquitous, *has it been that long*, issue. Are you kidding me? These clowns are shameless. When these magazines run out of naked chicks to put on the cover they go back to Biggie and Tupac. What's next, a Biggie and Tupac cooking issue?

These wannabe famous, wannabe hard core, prep school educated, Hampton hopping scribes that have spent about as much time in the 'hood as George W. Bush are co-conspirators in the absolute destruction of the image of positive Black men. Who but these trust fund babies could live off of the pittance that freelance magazine writers make to conduct the same Hip Hop interview over and over and over again?

Every *Vibe* and *Source* rapper interview can be summed up as follows: *'So, (insert rapper) have you sold drugs, done time, dropped out of high school, slapped a woman or had babies out of wedlock?'* They are so creative. This could only come from people with so little experience in the hood that they are seduced into painting one-dimensional portraits of some of the least interesting characters on the block.

Hip Hop magazines' pages are filled with story after hard luck story of young Black men who profess to be inches from returning to their bullet riddled past. If Hip Hop magazines' commitments to making sure that the suburbanites are deathly afraid of our boys could be contained to the Biggie Tupac thing, maybe we'd let them off the hook, but it doesn't end there. Suge Knight, Death Row Record's CEO, got out of jail and rappers Mystikal, C-Murder and Lil' Kim being in prison are the types of main events that their covers are set up for. Aren't these supposed to be music mags? Aren't these magazines supposed to be on our side? It doesn't feel like it.

They look more like glossy police blotters.

Let Time Magazine run just one issue of this crap and we'd call them every kind of racist imaginable. Jesse Jackson and other civil rights relics would be outside of their headquarters singing, crying and calling for boycotts. Essence, Ebony and Jet magazines have been the high watermark for positive Black images. At times they are so committed to the positive that objectivity is lost, but give me this over the choppy writing and lopsided presentations of the absolute worst images that the Hip Hop community has to offer. It does not matter if White people or Black people piss on your leg and tell you that it's raining. The results are the same.

Hard jawed little boys and their androgynous looking female rapping counterparts are positioned like gangster mannequins every single month to sell clothes, cars, rims, records, ring tones, porn websites, fake gold teeth and the imagery of ruthless dangerous Black people. There is no upside to the unevenly negative depiction of what these magazines do. Karma is theirs to behold as, after a decade of pimping Black boys, they have begun to reap what they sewed.

Isn't it ironic, that after peddling so much death between their pages, neither the Source nor Vibe can have awards shows to celebrate themselves without the threat or reality of violence and death being present? Just like it was back in 1997 when Biggie was murdered leaving one of their parties.

Would the two rappers have said what they said if they knew that it would cost them their lives? Would they have danced to the same old rapper interview if they knew that their words would infuriate the insane to kill them? Aren't we struggling with more complicated issues than the under prepared overzealous interviewers were capable of understanding? Was it all worth it?

One can only wonder about the two boys' eternal regrets. Would they have chosen to die so young because of what they said? One thing is clear and that is that the Biggie, second of the two rappers to die in a hail of bullets, wanted out. He candidly spoke in a televison interview shortly after Tupac's shooting. Remorse and fear was apparent in his words and posture. Slouched over, Biggie spoke deliberately and glowingly about his rap rival Tupac. He reflected on their friendship, mutual artistic respect and attempted to even add context to their musical feud. Biggie used the interview to call for an end to the violence. He did what everyone ultimately does, he blamed it all on the media, and this time he was right. He said he wanted to live. He wanted the violence to stop, presumably before it got to him.

Unfortunately, the mold had been cast. Biggie had said too much. The sun was setting in the barnyard and both Biggie and Tupac had signed up to be thugs. It was there, as a self-proclaimed, drug dealing, gun-toting thug where he would die.

This chapter of Hip Hop's thug life left two mothers without their sons. In the case of Christopher Wallace, the Notorious B.I.G., there's a wife and two more Black children without a husband and father. In both cases the community is robbed of the opportunity to experience what could have been once these two boys realized that you can't invite death in because it will seize the invitation.

The Hip Hop community is a closed society. It cannot be changed from the outside. We have to change it or it and us, like Biggie and 'Pac, will die.

Enough is enough

We have made too many excuses for thugs and the foolishness that defines them. We have treated their antics as entertainment while overlooking the far-reaching implications of the destruction that we reap as a result of the poison that they sew. Can you love a thug? Obviously. How do you? Now that's more complex.

These indifferent little boys do need love. More love than most people are willing or have to give. They need pure, honest, strong and structured love. Agape. This is the same type of love that Dr. Martin Luther King, Jr. spoke of when he said that he loved this country. He said that he loved this nation so much that he was willing to die to make it right. This is the kind of love that says to every single one of our little thugs in training that I love you, but hate what you do. This love says, as long as you do what you are doing to destroy our community and yourself, you have got to go. If you continue, I love you so much that I will call the police on you and ensure that you are prosecuted to the letter of the law if that is what it will take to save your life and the lives that you will touch.

Heal this brotha'!

It's not the intrinsic value of life's experiences that define us. It's how we respond to them. Life is hard. That's it. People disappoint. Fathers don't father, mothers don't mother, teachers don't teach and we all have to deal with it. People lie, sometimes for our own good, other times for their own good, then other times for no good reason. Being born is not the challenge, nor is dying. It's the process between that is difficult.

Life, no matter who we are, gives us two choices, always.

We can take what we have been given and use it to improve our lot or we can look at what we have as insufficient, quit and start trying to take other people's stuff. The choices are truly simple.

Children want to be led. They want somebody to tell them what love is, how to tie a tie, what colors go together, how to study for math, where they come from, which friends are best, and what it feels like to be safe and loved. They can figure out how to grill cheese, to kiss and where to put their hands when they're dancing, but that doesn't mean that we, the adults, are not painfully necessary. Connecting to a child is the beginning. Directing them and giving them the opportunity to be kids is what will save them.

For thugs to be helped, they have to open up their hearts and minds and allow themselves to be led in a direction that is new, different and positive. For us to lead them out of their despair, we have to be positive people worth following. If we intend to connect to and then lead them, we cannot present ourselves as perfect anymore than we can wallow in the foolish decisions of our youth. We must be stand-up men and women who admit to stumbling daily and struggling to keep our balance.

Our boys need self-esteem. Committed adults can help bring that about. By middle school a series of caring adults are the first and last lines of defense to save our kids from the streets. Connecting them to a solid peer group is another method of saving our boys from a life on the bottom.

Thugs in waiting have the worst time finding and staying connected to good kids. The good kids want more than their neighborhood has to offer even if they live in a palace. Good kids know that there is a big world out there and they want a piece of it. Being a good kid isn't about grades. It's attitude. Good kids listen to caring adults about 41% of the time, on a good day. The rest of the time they do what all kids do, listen to their friends or their heart.

The problem with bringing good kids and bad kids together is that the good kids are often wrestling with the challenges of being good, when good isn't cool. Good and bad boys are simultaneously trying to establish their sense of self. The stronger the child's self-esteem the more likely they are to pull away from negativity. Self-esteem is built through steady affirming relationships with adults and peers. These relationships are most easily developed with steady adults who have created a reliable and supportive lifestyle.

Troubled boys need to be in environments where even being bad doesn't mean illegality. This could mean that the parent(s) has to move. The move may not be comfortable for the family, but the alternative is even more uncomfortable. One of the most important things a parent can do for their child is to remove decisions. Don't let a kid think that he has a choice in whether he's going to school, going to listen to the teacher, or do his homework. Don't let him think that he has a choice to do things that will be bad for him. Love him and if that doesn't work, get medieval on his butt.

Teach him follow through. So what he doesn't like his coach. His coach may not like him either. And? Your boss probably doesn't like you. And? We have to teach our kids that the world is not theirs to bend rules as they see fit. They must also learn that when they do bend the rules that there are consequences and repercussions. Our kids cannot cast aside the uncomfortable parts of living anymore than we can. The sooner they learn this the easier they will be to raise, educate and get out of the house. The more adroit they are at following through, the more effective they will be at finishing college or trade school, holding down a job, starting a

55

business, raising kids and ultimately taking care of you. So he will finish out the basketball season, not because basketball is important, but because following through is.

Finally, there is no substitute for good parenting. It is not a panacea, but it sure makes everything else easier. Your child is your social life. Would-be thugs have a penchant for finding the worst that an environment has to offer. This is why parents must be diligent, stay involved and remember that they are parents first. Even as teens, kids act like infants. Sure, they look grown and think that they are grown, but they are babies. Kids need parental guidance. They need us to keep an eye on them. Just like when they were toddlers, when you can't see or hear them, they probably have a hand full of Vaseline. So keep them in your sight. This just means knowing where they are or should be at all times. Even the worst parent has no excuse now that there are cell phones with cameras. These devices erase excuses for not knowing where your kids are at all times.

Structure your son's time. If he is involved in supervised structured activities, you improve the probability of him staying focused and finding a purpose. This means that you and he should be involved with something during the summer, fall, winter and spring until he goes to college. You have to support him in his activities. Go to all of your kid's games, participate in the booster club and, if you haven't done it yet, get your education.

'Do as I say' is some old bull. If you want your son to succeed in education, show him what success in education looks like by being successful in it. One can't help but wonder if that mother we see every summer on the TV news crying over her dead son ever went to any of his parent/teacher nights. Be there for the best that your son has to offer and there will likely be more good times than bad.

Drastic times call for drastic measures

Politics, organized labor and our inattentive communities have maintained the conditions in today's urban schools. As our kids get force fed failing urban schools, what would be interesting to see is how many urban teachers send their kids to their employing school. But since we don't know this interesting little tidbit, did you ever wonder where politicians' kids go to school? Well let's take a look.

Congress must know something about the public schools that the rest of us don't. An article in the *Hartford Courant* recently reported that, while over 90% of Americans that send their kids to public schools, most of our national leaders do not.

The article reported that 46% of the Republican Senate have their kids in private school. Oh, but chill ye of Democratic faith, 52% of your senators have opted out of a free American education. Now hold on one minute. Don't you start thinking that this is a White thing. Black or Hispanic legislators ain't sending their kids to their district's public schools either. Just look at the Congressional Black and Hispanic Caucuses. Black legislators take their kids out of district schools at a rate of 29%, while 46% of the Hispanic legislators have ushered their children out of public schools.

Congress knows that, although for profit and not for profit, agencies live and die by their ability to produce. They don't expect this of big 'ol urban schools. Because their kids ain't in 'em, they can let our schools fail for generations with little more penalty than a new leader.

Politicians have no problem putting the construction of schools out to bid to private firms. Why not give the school district's central office more opportunities to recognize educational leaders by rewarding them with the chance to open or reorganize public schools? Make the bidding competitive, the compensation adequate, and the monitoring extensive. Talented teachers and administrators will thrive in these settings. The less skilled will be forced to realize what we all have had to learn when we learned that our dreams of being professional athletes were just that - dreams. Everybody can't do every job. Some teachers just can't teach.

Vouchers, magnets, charters and independents all need to be put on the table. Leave the politics out of this. OUR KIDS ARE DYING A MILLION DEATHS! We need hope. We need change. We need competition right now! With large-scale competition all educators would enter the real world economy. Just like attorneys, accountants, auto mechanics and hairdressers, teachers could become year round employees who have to show their clients that they have earned the right to work. This is not a call for capricious firings of excellent or even good teachers or administrators. It is a call for equity. It is a call for teachers and administrators to tie their careers to those of the children that they are entrusted to educate. It is a call for a new day in education. This new day is one in which children are no longer forced into the cycle of poverty by virtue of their zip code.

Who could argue for a non-competitive failing educational system? What person in their right mind could honestly and openly defend generations of failure that have so disproportionately crushed the dreams of one group? Is there an empathetic individual alive who could be against giving the most talented and committed among us access to public money to save all of our children? Even prisons have gone private. The last good school has not been built.

Stop whining about money. According to NCES, urban schools get as much, if not more, than their suburban counterparts. Yes, we know, there are more problems in the urban schools. That's what we are trying to fix. Concentrating poverty in one school is what we are trying to change. Just like when public housing projects were dismantled and traded for Section 8 vouchers to disperse the poverty, the same can and must be done for schools.

It's not about resources. It's about rethinking. There are still thousands walking through the dreams of caring professionals from across the nation. These people want a chance to help save our kids. Let's invite them in. Let's work together. Let the failing schools close and in their place, let us begin anew. Let's dream big and open small. The achievement gap does not have to become a permanent stain on the future of this generation.

Thugs exist and thrive because of bad decisions by the adults and the kids. School and homes can be improved so that we can provide our boys with more options that don't include violence and crime. We have the power, especially in our communities, to improve the offerings. Our schools do have enough money, we just need better places to spend it. Our homes do have enough love. We just need better ways to show it and our leaders will follow us if we show them that we care about our boys and the way they represent us.

Man up

Fatback, 40 oz. and Fornication
Chapter 3

Born to die

"Most Black men have not seen the inside of a doctor's office by age 45," declares Washington Hospital Center's Dr. Elizabeth Nelson. Dr. Nelson, a Howard University Medical School graduate, practices internal medicine in the Washington, D.C. hospital whose patients are almost always Black and rarely male. She says that when Black men do see a doctor, "They are in the ER where perhaps, incidentally, hypertension or diabetes are discovered." Dr. Nelson joins the chorus of sources that report that

Black men live the shortest, unhealthiest lives of both genders and all racial groups.

"Black men suffer from far worse health conditions than any other racial group in America," according to Jerry Kennard of the online journal Men's Health, (menshealth.about.com). The journal states that Black men live 7.1 years less than all other racial groups. *Men's Health* says that 44% of us are overweight and 24% of Black men are considered obese. The journal goes on to say that Black men's rate of prostate cancer is the highest in the nation. When considering all forms of cancer, Kennard says that the five year survival rate for African-Americans diagnosed between 1986-1992 was only 44% compared with 59% for White Americans. Black men have incidences of diabetes that are about 70% higher than White Americans, Kennard concludes. Black, plus male, equals unhealthy.

The U.S. Center for Disease Control and Prevention (CDC) reports that Black infants are twice as likely to die as White ones. When none of this works to snuff us out, we kill ourselves, literally. Suicide rates continue to be of great concern for African-American males according to the National Institute for Mental Health. From cradle to grave, being Black and male is inherently risky.

Living dangerously

Our eating, drinking and sexual habits are evidence that Black Americans have mounted an all out assault on ourselves. Between our extraordinary rate of homicide, 57.8 per 100,00 versus 5.1 per 100,000 for White men, and the impact of often-preventable conditions such as heart disease and HIV/AIDS, nobody kills more Black men than Black men, according to the National Institute for

Mental Health. Our multi-dimensional mass suicide is aided by our culture and abetted by ignorance. Our basic cultural tendencies are at the root of our unhealthiness.

Black people seemed to have developed a mantra, 'the more lethal something, is the more willing we are to consume it.' At some point dangerous and dumb will have to be handed off to another group. Living healthy is about using some basic common sense.

Black people, especially Black men, have to realize that it is not a sign of Black pride to eat the least healthiest food, drink the largest quantities of hard liquor, or run raw through the bushes. These are dumb and dangerous activities that have become cultural tendencies. Be clear, African-Americans are not alone when it comes to the aforementioned or unmentioned behavioral shortcomings. We are human and therefore we err. We are, however, the most negatively impacted by these behaviors. Until we redefine what behaviors classify us as Black, we will continue to legally and gleefully neglect our health and shorten our lives. Our pride in the perpetuation of dangerous and dumb habits is killing millions of Black people every year.

Those of us who know better are unwilling to change our habits because we are too committed to 'keepin' it real,' which translates into dying young. Eating light, drinking less, and having safer sex is akin to being 'soft.' A real Black man with steamed veggies, one glass of wine and a condom? Please…

What's for dinner

Everything from environmental racism to traditions of nutritional exclusion have led to the creation of African-American eating habits that have clogged our hearts and shot our blood pressure through the roof. Add to this an inverted sexism, which makes men think that men don't go to the doctor, and we see how Black men's health risks skyrocket.

What did you eat last night? This is a question that more and more loved ones need to ask our brothas. We value greasy food more than life itself. We hang cheap meat around our necks like a fat gold chain.

We want our food to drip with fat. Anything less would be absurd. So we collect the used grease in empty coffee cans, then line the back of our ovens. The only caution given to this practice is making sure to put the fish grease in the fish grease can versus pouring it into the pig grease can. Now that would be a problem.

Imagine a soul food restaurant that dared to serve Black people skinless baked chicken. There would be a riot. Black people would organize to shut down the treasonous culinary infiltrators.

"They ain't really Black," would be the charge we'd raise against the rebel restaurateurs. The grounds for pulling their Black membership card would be the question, "Who would take the skin off of chicken?" Then minutes before the gathered angry mob readied to burn to the ground the skinless chicken bakers, a breathless fat Black man would run in to report, "KFC is now open 'til midnight!" A roar would erupt as grown men would embrace, knowing that they could still get a five piece dark, with macaroni and fake cheese, potatoes smothered in gravy and beautiful white biscuits until midnight. Desperate diet dodgers would turn their hats backwards and take off in a childish sprint toward the sanctuary of clogged arteries. Jubilant protesters would break down with real tears of victory as others walked off entranced by their stomach's muscle memory of the Colonel's 12 secret herbs and spices, floating in the amber glows of popping grease vats. Relieved that our sacred bird will not be subjected to an undignified skinless baked memorial, greasy hands would join in singing Negro hymns, *We shall overcome some daaaaay...*

Look man, as a ham eating, candied yam loving, five cheese macaroni and cheese devouring, collard greens smothered in as much meat as the pot will hold kind-a-brotha, I feel your pain. This is not about abstinence. It's not about becoming health experts either. Hell, it's not even about fundamental change. We are discussing curtailing conscious consumption. We are focusing on moderation. So relax and step away from the table. Put down your 32 oz. grape soda with no ice and just chill. Let's see if we can help you live.

Why do we need so much fast food

What in the hell is the hurry? We inject our families with so much of this crap that our kids are overflowing a heap of grown ass fat out of their skintight Baby Phat jeans. Look at our high schools. They're overrun with overweight inactive kids. Seventeen year old kids with guts, real honest to goodness guts, are lumbering through the halls of Anytown, USA. Our teens have traded in the pubescent six packs for middle aged kegs.

"Consuming non-diet soda and fruit juices that have high sugar and calories in them could cause our kids to gain as much as 10 to 15 pounds in a year," Dr. Nelson claims. She says that kids are fatter today than they were ten years ago and it's because of what and when they are eating. Dr. Nelson admits that "Kids are eating dinner very late and between the heavy meals they go to sleep within two hours or less of eating." Eating bad, heavy and late along with the kids' inactivity makes them fat and at risk of becoming unhealthy adults who will struggle with obesity and its accompanying dangers.

Our mouths, our decision

When it comes to what and how we eat, there's nobody to blame anymore but us. We are sadly passing on our horrible eating habits to our kids. Every time that we steer into a Popeye's Famous Chicken with a gaggle of children so classically conditioned that the smell of frying poultry makes them drool like one of Pavlov's dogs, we make our kids' lives shorter and less healthy. When we are summoned by a Big Mac attack or lead yet another pilgrimage to an all-you-can-eat Chinese buffet, we are promising our kids that they will live lives riddled with early and severe health risks.

If you think kids look older now than they did when we were younger, it's because they do. Fat makes people look older, especially kids. When these kids who are 20 plus pounds overweight are walking around in clothes that don't fit, we should have serious cause for pause. In our children we see what just the first 15 years of horrible eating habits looks like.

We have to rewrite our family's menu or there will be no one with whom we will be having dinner. We have so misled our kids on eating that they think that Red Lobster and Sizzler are fine dining. If you concur with your child's poorly trained and misguided pallet, then Houston, we have a problem.

We can eat better and here's how

Brothas, we look like a flaming hot mess. If looking bad were the only problem, then we'd be all right, but it's not. The outside is a tamed image of what is happening on the inside. We are unhealthy, largely because we choose to be. Just as we have chosen a short road to a quick death through our habits of consumption, we can change direction and choose a long road to a long life. The short road is paved with snacks and pork rinds. The long one is full of whole fresh fruit.

We can eat better. We don't have to gorge ourselves of the worst cuts of red meat anymore. Nor do we have to smother every meal in some sort of gravy. No longer do we need to eat everything on a pig including, but not limited to, the ears, nose, intestines, feet, knuckles, and the oink itself. It's not cheaper to eat like this, just more dangerous. It's even harder to prepare this diet than let's say, baking a chicken. Estimated prep time for cooking chitterlings? An entire afternoon. Estimated cost of a bucket of chitterlings? $10. Seven chicken breasts? $8. Positive impact of eating better.... Priceless.

Your decision to eat hog intestines will give you the dubious distinction of spending the next few days living in a house and wearing clothes that smell like a public bathroom. Yeah, yeah, yeah, not in your house because you know how to clean 'em... but why? Even after they are cooked with every imaginable spice to disguise the flavor, you still have to drench these pig guts in hot sauce and stick 'em between a hand-full of white bread to trick your gag reflex. The only upside to eating this mess is that it will kill you quicker so the smell won't bother you for long. Leave "Fear Factor" to crazy maggot eating women with fake breasts. Put down the hot sauce and step away from the jar of sweet tea and nobody is gonna get hurt.

Leave the nostalgia for people who don't know any better. Welcome to the First World brothas. Look around. We have supermarkets here with aisle after well-lit aisle of healthy choices for both lunch and dinner. Take your time. Walk around a bit. See what else they have. These places are marvelous. This is a wonderful country isn't it?

Black people love fattening food so much that we have even taken the most benign meat of all, turkey, and made it a holiday death trap. Who on earth fries, no deep-fries a 15 pound animal? It's like dropping a full-sized poodle in a pot. Oh right, I almost forgot, if it ain't dangerous it ain't Black. Well then, allow me to introduce you to your deep fried 'thugged out' Thanksgiving.

In recent years many Black families have adopted a new holiday ritual of frying an entire turkey. As unbelievable as it sounds to those who've never witnessed it, we turn this bird into a 15-pound fat greasy sponge and think nothing of it. In fact, tripling the fat content of turkey is sort of revelatory.

'We'll show them! The Man can't trick us into eating light. We'll celebrate Thanksgiving as strong Black men.' So we stand outside in the dead of winter, risking life and limb trying to figure out how to cook with the propane fueled deep fryer, the most dangerous home cooking device on the market.

The sheer joy of beating The Man sends a sense of pride rushing through the home. The women folk hurry about pressing their faces to the iced window anticipating how tender the meat is going to be. They gaze upon the valiant shivering chefs as hunters. They applaud as their husbands lose their eyebrows to the flames and hot grease. The men folk fight flames and winter just so that the family can keep their fat content on full blast. As the men stand around the bubbling silver pot, under an umbrella freezing their nuts off they have the 'I've done something good' smile frozen to their faces. *It's turkey, y'all*. Dry ass turkey. It's not chicken. It's not ham. Turkey. This bird is almost entirely white meat. Let it go. It's supposed to be dry.

We sacrifice good sense so that our bodies don't go into a low fat detox. Can you see it? Imagine a holiday in which we thought beyond the gluttony of stuffing the dinner table and ourselves full of as much fat and sodium as we can conjure? Think about a holiday when we celebrate and ate healthy.

Black folks, we seem to be losing our minds as we fight to wriggle ourselves free of this almost unnatural state of health conscientiousness. It'd be Easter Sunday and to keep our sodium levels high both the grown-ups' and kids' tables would be dealing salt packets like corner pushers. 'Yo, I got some Lawry's... Psst, I got a stick of butter...' Grandma would be cussing because grandpa would still be awake after dinner. Then we glance over into the living room to see our Uncle Tyrone cowering in the corner, lightheaded, because he could actually feel his arteries unclogging.

What and how we eat can be fixed and our lives saved. If we don't change our habits, we will soon become worm food.

Dying of culture

Our hearts are stopping because we are clogging them up with culture. Here's a simple biology lesson. Your heart stops, you die. Let's move on.

According to the American Heart Association, heart disease

claims the lives of 100,000 Black people a year. That is every single year, at least 100,000 Black Americans die from heart disease. Said differently, Black people are suffering a death toll similar to the 2005 Southeast Asian tsunami or the tragedy of New Orleans' hurricane Katrina year after year. At least with the tsunami there was fan fair and a star-studded telethon. When the cause is heart disease we just die in silence.

Due to heredity and lifestyle, heart disease and strokes present a serious threat to African-Americans because we have a high incidence of certain risk factors, such as high blood pressure. Heart disease accounts for a third of deaths among African-American men according to the CDC.

Heart disease usually occurs when a person has high levels of cholesterol, a fat-like substance, in the blood. Fried, basted, braised, au gratin, crispy, escalloped, pan-fried, sautéed, stewed or stuffed foods are high in fat. Regular consumption of food prepared this way will increase our probability of developing heart disease. If you are enjoying this thing called life, you might want to start looking for some steamed, broiled, baked, grilled, poached or roasted foods.

Another contributor to heart disease is high sodium foods. So on your trek through the supermarket walk past the Ramen Noodles and shimmy by the canned foods, because eating too much of these high sodium delicacies could shoot your blood pressure through the roof. Other foods high in sodium include those that are pickled, in cocktail sauce, smoked, in broth or au jus, in a tomato base, or in soy or teriyaki sauce. If you're not sure about something you ordered at Ponderosa, ask your server how it's prepared. If that doesn't work, bring your tail home and cook, because the food in restaurants usually has so much sodium that you don't even need to ask. Remember, it's about changing habits of consumption and fighting negative tendencies of the community. So go home, sit down and eat with your kids, maybe even talk to them, as opposed to handing bags of food to them in the back seat as you tear out of the drive-thru.

On the average, high blood cholesterol, high blood pressure and smoking doubles your chance of developing heart disease. Therefore, a person who has all three risk factors is far more likely to develop heart disease than someone who has none. Remember, heart disease, plus Black people equals 100,000 deaths annually. Traditional African-American diets often lead to high blood cholesterol and high blood pressure. Then when smoking is added, the reasons why so many Black people die of heart disease becomes very clear.

Obesity and physical inactivity are other factors that can lead to heart disease. Being overweight increases the likelihood of developing high blood cholesterol and high blood pressure, and physical inactivity increases the risk of heart attack. If you think that you might be overweight, you probably are. Most of us are. You're not big boned brotha'. There are no fat skeletons, just fat people. Dr. Nelson says that regular exercise is required if we want to be healthy. This means at least 30 minutes of exercise three times weekly because 30 minutes of activity gets your heart rate up high and long enough to constitute aerobic exercise. However, the bottom line is that if you consume more calories than you burn, then you will gain, not lose weight. A glass does not empty when you continue to fill it and neither will you.

The process of clogging our arteries begins in most people

during childhood, continues through the teenage years and worsens, as we get older. It is never too early to start eating right. We can and must train our kids to eat better by helping them to adapt to a healthy diet that includes foods that are low in sodium and fat. Overall good nutrition and smoking cessation is essential to controlling the risk factors for heart disease and making possible a longer healthier life.

Pour some out for my homies

Since when did we start carrying around a whole bottle and drinking it ourselves? Black people are the only group for whom it has been found that there are no, yes I repeat, no positive effects of alcohol consumption on our health. This is part of what researchers call a "J-shaped" relationship. For many ethnic groups moderate drinkers show a lower mortality risk than lifetime abstainers from alcohol, while heavy drinkers show a higher mortality risk than both moderate drinkers and abstainers. In some racial groups there is a point at which drinking in moderation is actually good for their health. Unfortunately, none of these groups are African-Americans. Drinking is both a physical and cultural problem for Black people.

Black people start drinking earlier than any other racial group of Americans, according to the CDC. The CDC reports that the racial group with the highest percentage of kids who drank before the age of 13 is African-Americans, 31%.

Although the CDC says that African-Americans have the lowest reports of alcoholism, we are the least likely to receive treatment when it does occur. This could be one of the reasons why there are lower reports of Black alcoholism. Failure to seek or participate in treatment is another example of Black men's lack of attention to our health. Brothas, what is the deal? What has happened to us that makes us so adverse to treatment even when the health issue is something as destructive as alcoholism? When are we going to shed this foolish fear of being perceived as soft?

Alcoholism is another example of the need for both personal and governmental change. We need more affordable and accessible treatment for alcoholism. We also have to be honest with ourselves as Black men. Definitions abound for what constitutes an alcoholic. What is more important than defining alcoholism for us is requiring that we look at our lives and decide if our drinking has a positive impact on it.

Running raw

We Black men have to change our sexual habits. The way we have sex is killing us at higher rates than what we eat or drink, homicide, car accidents or natural disasters. Among the top four leading killers of Black men ages 25-44 is AIDS according to the United States Center for Disease Control.

Our extraordinarily high rates of contraction of this dreaded disease do not affect us alone. We are passing it on to Black women so much that the highest incidence of growth among AIDS cases in the United States is among heterosexual Black women. AIDS is the leading cause of death for Black women ages 25-44. According to the CDC, 59.9% of all women living with HIV/AIDS are Black.

Again, your pain is deeply felt. There are few men who don't enjoy the sensation of a sexual encounter. There is literally no other feeling like it. Chris Rock said that there is nothing like unwrapping a new sexual partner. (Okay, I cleaned it up. It's Chris

Rock. I had to.) True. There is also almost nothing more dangerous to Black men than sex. Driving without seatbelts, playing with knives or running with scissors are all less risky to Black men 25-44 than having unprotected sex. I cannot say it enough that various sources claim that AIDS is a leading cause of death among African-American men ages 25-44 and is the number one cause of death for Black women in the same age group.

This is not a moral call. Adam had a problem listening to God and so do we. Think about it, Adam was told to leave Eve alone by the Lord himself and still his libido won out. Abstinence is a tall mountain to climb, so most of us chose the hills of careful partner selection as a means of protection. Unfortunately by the time we can see AIDS, it's too late. Therefore, the selection method is by no means effective.

None of us are safe enough to point an accusing finger at people who have contracted AIDS. The attraction of sex, especially the unprotected variety, has put us all at risk.

If you have ever had unprotected sex, you could have been exposed to HIV, the virus that causes AIDS. Even if you have never had unprotected sex, don't kid yourself into thinking that your 'protection' was foolproof. There is no level of numeration or formula that makes you safe. One exposure is all that is required to contract this horrible disease. Even if you have been careful, this does not mean that you know what your partner has done. So to everyone who has ever had oral, vaginal or anal sex at least once, welcome to the AIDS risk pool. Now let's get down to business.

More than any other health issue, AIDS is a blind indiscriminate killer that is ravaging our community. Colon and other cancers, while deadly, if detected early, can often be cured. AIDS, even if discovered minutes after contraction, cannot be cured. At best it can be treated, but there is no known cure for HIV/AIDS.

This virus, more than any other issue discussed anywhere in this book, is more likely to kill off Black men because it plays on our carnal weaknesses. Unprotected sex, multiple partners, and drug use are all primary causes of the spread of AIDS. They all are also habits too prevalent in the Black community. It is frighteningly clear that the sum of our habits creates a behavioral predisposition for Black men to contract and die from HIV/AIDS.

As painful as it is to admit, AIDS is a killer that we inject into ourselves and those with whom we are most intimate. Passage of these high-risk behaviors on to the next generation has already occurred. African-American children represent 62.7% of all pediatric AIDS cases in the United States, yet our kids make up just 12% of the population, according to the CDC National Prevention Information Network.

You know someone with HIV/AIDS

Blacks, and our running partners Latinos, together comprise 60% of the nearly 900,000 cases of AIDS in the U.S. reported to the CDC since the epidemic took hold in 1981. Latinos' infection rates are consistent with their percentage of the population, 19% of them are infected and they make up 13% of the population. African-Americans make up 12% of the population according to the U.S. Census Bureau and we swell the group of those infected. African-Americans account for 49.3% of all AIDS cases reported in the United States in 2003. This bears repeating. African-Americans account for only 12% of the people living in the U.S. and we account for 49.3% of the country's AIDS cases.

With this disease taking out nearly as many young Black men than violence and cancer, it's all too likely that you know someone with HIV/AIDS. The infected are people we love, work with and have seen at the club, go to school with and ride the bus with. Unless we plan on having unprotected sex with them, their HIV/AIDS status does not put our family or us in any danger. Let them live. Don't chase them out of our churches or their jobs, keep them in our family and support them as best we can. Think of how you would like to be treated and then extend that same compassion to them. If we are their friends, then we have likely done what they did to contract the virus. People hang with people like themselves. So y'all were doing the same things and maybe even the same women. You got lucky, for now. We are all in the risk pool.

Starting young and dumb

How many 25 to 44 year olds are contracting sexually transmitted diseases at such high rates becomes clear when we consider Black men's very early, highly active and dangerous sexual habits. Many of our boys are having sex BEFORE they turn 13. According to the CDC while only 5% of White males in 2003 had sex before they were 13, 32% of Black boys were. These are boys barely past playing Little League baseball, are making life and death decisions. Do you want an 8th grader creating life or contracting a certain death?

Even if all of these boys are not getting infected with HIV/AIDS, many of them are getting little girls pregnant. This is a sure sign that they are in fact having unprotected sex at alarming numbers. Out of wedlock teen birth rates for African-Americans ages 15 to 19 remains at 85 births per 1,000 women, almost double the rate for

White teens, 45 births per 1,000 women, according to a study published by Johns Hopkins Bloomberg School of Public Health. Yet again, even though the Census counts us as just 12% of the population in the US, our kids accounted for 23% of all of the teen births in United States in 1995.

Our kids are getting each other pregnant and spreading diseases, but you knew that already. We all knew that. If no one ever dropped another statistic about Black teens and pregnancy, you could comfortably say that you know that there is an epidemic in the Black community that starts with unprotected sex.

Fifteen year-old parents have somehow become the least of our concerns. We crowd into state sponsored maternity rooms, balloons in hand, trying to act like there is nothing strange about two children who can't get a driver's license or work in most states becoming parents. We are over the girl's unwillingness to wait a week before she takes her child in to the high school that she will not graduate from for show and tell. We're cool with the baby's first gold name chain, Nike sweat suit and Timberland boots. Somehow this bizarre scene has become normal. Like people living in a war zone desensitized to the violence, Black families are collectively unphased by Black children having unprotected sex, getting pregnant and having babies. We don't consider for a second that the mother, father and baby may all die of AIDS within five years.

Teen pregnancy blends into our community like an elephant. Many of us hate the bad decision and love the child. It is understandable and necessary to some extent, that once the decision has been made by the child to have a child, (doesn't that sound crazy to you?)… anyway, once the child has decided to have the child, somebody has got to take care of both the child and the infant.

So what ends up happening is that the adults accept responsibility to take care of both the teen mother and her child while overlooking the obvious. This time the unprotected sex led to life, next time it could spell death.

Uneducated, unprotected sex has led to a health crisis in the Black community. The babies that our babies are making are twice as likely to have a low birth weight and 1.5 times as likely to be premature than White babies according to the same Johns Hopkins' study. When our kids have unprotected, uneducated sex, they are putting themselves and their babies at risk.

While there are other contributing factors to the specific spread of HIV/AIDS, including men who have unprotected sex with men, it is too easy and inaccurate, to put the pandemic of AIDS on brothas on the down low. Heterosexual transmissions are steadily rising with no end in sight. Remember, heterosexual Black women, who are having sex with Black men, are the group with the highest rate of HIV/AIDS acquisition.

Wake up

Monogamy and abstinence are lofty, rarely achieved goals. Statistics abound about divorce rates. Some have 50% of marriages splitting while others move the number higher. This number has no bearing on how many frogs get kissed even before marriage.

Dating can be a feverish time in one's life. The number of partners for many women and men before they marry could and do often average in high teens and twenties. Sorry to break it to you brothas, she isn't just talented, it's the result of trial and error. So yes, somebody taught her that. By the time the white dress is donned, a whole bunch of sex has typically taken place for the bride and groom. Then, among those relationships that are together, researchers and therapists agree on only one thing, very few married people are faithful for the full duration of the relationship.

People are having sex with more than one person, regularly. Still again, to find out just how much sex is being had by Black people, we need only to go back to our young boys. Just as our kids are representations of our families' nutritional and community values, they are also examples of how we feel about sex. Kids do what parents tolerate and apparently in 2004 we tolerated 42% of our Black male teens having sex with four or more partners, according to the CDC. This almost quadruples the sexual activity of White boys during the same period of time, 12%, according to the CDC.

Where did they learn this? Trust, it wasn't a rap video, the media or the school. Ignorance has primed the Black community for the spread of HIV/AIDS. Ignorance accompanied by homophobia, guided twisted interpretations of religion are shutting our mouths and opening our kids' legs.

We teach our kids our values and in the voids of our teachings, the kids try to figure it out themselves. The results are painful and scary. Our children have the most children and contract AIDS at the highest rates.

Talk to your kids about sex. Be there for their questions. Learn the answers together.

HIV/AIDS is here

HIV/AIDS will affect every single one of us in one way or another. According to the CDC, we are contracting this virus at rates five times that of White people. At the very least this disease should get us to change the way we have sex. Those of us who have contracted the disease cannot be cast aside as dirty promiscuous beasts, homosexuals or drug addicts. Nice people get AIDS too. Rich and famous people will suffer alongside the poor and anonymous until we put aside the behavior and the prejudice so that we can come together to find a cure.

Whoever thinks that Hall of Fame basketball player and entrepreneur Ervin "Magic" Johnson and rapper EZ E are the last two famous Black men to contract HIV/AIDS is nuts. Think about it, for Black men 25 to 44 HIV/AIDS is one of the top killers. (Even as I write this time after time and read it even more, it is hard for me to accept, but it is true.) Professional athletes are almost exclusively Black, male and between the ages of 25 to 44. Along with their entertainer brothers, this group of men have developed a tradition of highly sexual and risky behaviors. Just watch MTV's *Cribs.* Look at how many of the rappers and athletes take you to their children's rooms. You, just like the rest of us, look for the photo of the wife, but there are none, just a string of baby's mammas, the result of unprotected sex; the same behavior that will give them HIV/AIDS.

If there were ever a group who should come out swinging by dumping every free dime that they were about to spend on jewelry and cars into research, it's professional athletes and entertainers. Magic is not the only one with HIV/AIDS y'all, he can't be. Wilt Chamberlain wasn't the last brotha to screw indiscriminately. Remember Kobe? According to various news reports he went up in a hotel employee raw dog. He'd just met her hours before and, as we later found out, she had had sex with three other men in three days. We know this because investigators say they found that she still had 'residue' from the other sexual encounters when they examined her. Kobe is lucky that all he got was caught.

College athletes are not immune either. The intersection of age, race and gender are predictors that say that Black college athletes are highly vulnerable to contracting this disease. There surely is more than just one good-looking Black athlete who, if tested, would find out that he too has HIV or AIDS. It is a numerical and behavioral impossibility that we have seen the last of the high profile HIV/AIDS cases. This is why all college and professional sports need to stop being punks and get in the AIDS cure business.

It's so convenient and necessary to visit hospitals with sick kids who have incommunicable diseases, but there is a pressing need to do something about AIDS. It might be unpopular to slam home the AIDS message in arena after arena, but that is where it is most needed. Black, sports loving men and the groupies who sweat them, (sorry about that ladies), need to keep AIDS at the front of their collective consciousness. The NBA, NFL, MLB and NCAA need to band together, take the billions that they are making worldwide and pump the pockets of AIDS labs full. Nike, get your butts over here too. You and Reebok, as well as any other footwear company, are spending billions to get little Black boys in your shoes. Dead kids stop buying sneakers. Make stopping the spread of HIV/AIDS your priority. The disease is killing your profits.

Historically Black colleges and universities, you too need to rise up. You are home to more 25 to 44 year old Black men and women than any other organization this side of the penitentiary. Make talking about HIV/AIDS second only to maintaining good grades. These often conservative God fearing institutions must join us all in this scary dark shadow of AIDS or this disease will do to African-Americans what it is doing to Africans, utter decimation.

HIV/AIDS will affect every one of us. We need to be more

compassionate of the infected. These are our brothers and sistas. Stop asking how they got it. Who cares? You know that it's contracted through unprotected sex, intravenous drug use or any other blood-to-blood relationship. Now that you know how everybody got it, let's move on and focus on finding a cure.

Come together right now

If there were ever an issue that must unite us it would have to be HIV/AIDS. This disease is more of a threat to us than drive-by shootings. Every year AIDS kills more people than all of those who perished in the 2001 World Trade Center attack. Yet there is no national outcry, no mobilization of troops, and no daily reports of casualties. Even if we stayed in Baghdad for another year, maintaining the current rate of death of our soldiers, AIDS would still kill more Black men during the same time period than the war on terror. We are in trouble and HIV/AIDS, as well as the behaviors that support it. We are all in the risk pool, which means that the life we save may be our own.

We have got to get tested and stay protected. God knows that getting tested is scary, but we have got to. Then we should treat everyone we even consider having any form of sex with like they are infected with something. If you can avoid having sex, then avoid it. If you are like the rest of us and you enjoy sex, and/or variety, stop by the store and pick up some latex condoms with the spermicidal gel nonoxinal 9. Then use them all of the time. Please.

Stop disease before it starts

Annual checkups and regular screenings for diabetes, colon and prostate cancer, as well as sexually transmitted diseases, are essential for everyone, especially Black men. Prevention is where we start to fall down. Putting on lotion in the morning does not constitute prevention. Dr. Nelson suggests, for instance, that by at age 40 men should have a digital rectal exam to evaluate them for signs of prostate cancer. She says though that convincing Black men to undergo the 15-minute painless, bloodless, potentially life saving exam is a huge problem because of our homophobia. 'Ain't nobody sticking his finger in my butt,' is the reason most often given. Instead of having a physician put a finger in our butt, we'd rather die of an often-preventable form of cancer. We are so tough.

M-O-D-E-R-A-T-I-O-N

Our food is killing us. Black men have to accept that we can't simply eat anything that we want. Alcoholism is killing us. We can't just drink as much as we want. Our sexual proclivities are killing us. We can't just have sex with whomever we want, even if it is protected. In the end it's our habits that are killing us.

African-American men in particular have developed decision and consumption habits that have laid the foundation for short unhealthy lives. In order to thwart self imposed genocide we have to find a way to bring into moderation our least talked about, most pervasive habits of eating, drinking and sex.

There is nothing more central to a community's survival than life itself. Improving the health of Black men is as much an individual issue as it is a community and national quagmire. African-American men's physical health is directly connected to the nation's social, economic and moral prosperity. Improving the length and quality of life of Black men, like all of the other issues discussed throughout this book, requires individual Black men, our community and nation to collaborate to develop long term solutions.

Lord, please protect us from us

When you clasp your hands together tonight, may I ask that you ask the Lord to protect us from us? No one is doing a better job killing Black men than Black men. Willingly, we eat the worst food. Happily, we consume some of the most potent liquor. Consensually, we have unprotected sex. Then we die in the millions. There is no more absolute truth than death. Both Black men and boys are committed to the most dangerous legal behaviors and for that we are dying. The only white sheets involved in this assault on the Black community are the ones used by the coroner to cover our decisions to forgo common sense. If there is a bright side to this it is that a brotha need only be equipped with common sense to choose moderation and protection to live longer and healthier. No degrees are needed, just a little common sense will save a lot of Black men.

Please say no to deadly behaviors and yes to life. We have used up all of our extra brothas. You are all that we have left. Please be moderate. Please.

The Reeducation of the Negro
Chapter 4

The big payback

The Black community sent us off to college. We turned that into a one-way ticket to the middle class. Their commitment to our becoming middle class allowed us to focus on us and we haven't looked back. Too many of us have found a strange solace and sense of belonging among the flocks of the newly minted disengaged Black middle-class. In this place we see ourselves as success stories and those left behind as victims of their own bad decisions.

In his 1933 landmark book *The Mis-Education of the*

Negro Dr. Carter G. Woodson sought to rally Black people, or Negroes, to play a major role in the salvation of our community. "One of the most striking evidences of the failure of higher education among Negroes is their estrangement from the masses, the very people upon whom they must eventually count for carrying out a program of progress, (Woodson, p. 52),"

Dr. Woodson's words are more poignant today than ever. Maybe this is why the *Mis-Education of the Negro* stays atop the Essence Best Sellers' paperback non-fiction list…that or lax accounting of sales receipts for other paperback non-fiction. No matter, if we employ Dr. Woodson's text as a conceptual frame for assessing educated Black people's contribution to the state of modern Black affairs, his words become so biting that it almost feels like he's insulting us; as he should. In his eyes, the success of our people was dependent upon the educated. Therefore, the Black community's failings are ours, especially if we have had individual success.

Were Dr. Woodson alive today we'd likely label him an outspoken conservative or maybe even a sell out for his consternation with educated Black people. Dead, he becomes another figure whose words sting has been soothed by the passing of time. So we're going to exhume the powerful intellectual and educator and cast his words against the backdrop of a community that is simultaneously growing poorer and richer.

We have left our community sitting on the steps of a segregated school waiting while our college-educated stay-at-home wives are busied with trips to ballet, piano and play dates. While our community's less accomplished and less fortunate wait, other communities come to pick up their elderly, poor and young, to lift them up. Dr. Woodson was not impressed with our selfish middle-class ascension. "The Negro forgets the delinquents of his race and goes his way to feather his own nest, (p.57)."

Our focus on us has blinded us. Our pursuit for respectability has transformed the purpose of prosperity. We were sent off to the middle class to improve the lot of us all. We got the improvement thing down, it's the 'us all' of which we have lost sight. Now, as much as ever, the Black community needs the accomplished to roll up our sleeves and engage in the process of finding solutions to the condition of Black America. Our failing schools, piss poor economy and minuscule political clout are resounding proof that the talented tenth has left ninety percent of the Black community with little more than scraps.

The same old Negro

Dr. Woodson's voice resonates throughout the pages of his perennial best-selling work. Even in 1933 it was clear to him that the Black middle class professionals should be the community's social architects. But then, like now, the Black professional class was splintered and its resources were shredded, thereby diminishing their usefulness in the struggle for self-determination.

In 1933 Dr. Woodson realized that, "The large majority of the educated Negroes who have put on the finishing touches of best colleges are all but worthless in the development of their people," (p. 2). He believed that we could build the institutions that establish the mores that set the foundation for our sustenance and eventual growth. Individuals as well as our professional and fraternal orders could own businesses, land and buildings within which they could devise curriculum and schools, museums and libraries, teachers and texts that tell our story to all who will listen.

The rope of affirmative action, once an escape route out of 400 years of butt whooping, is now around our necks. The long-term purpose of affirmative action has always been for those who benefit from it to pull others through briar patches of racism to the highest highs of professional advancement. Instead we have gotten caught up in the altitude. Without the support of those before us and those waiting to enter, we will hang in the tree of opportunity like strange fruit while White women and gay men dance their way to the top of the corporate ladder that we built. Until then, uneducated immigrants of every hue will continue to come into our communities and buy up everything that the White ethnics left behind.

Immigrants from all over the globe who don't even speak English are beating the snot out of the entire African-American community, especially the so-called Black middle and upper classes. Poor Black people have their own problems. The tragedy of the African American experience is most noticeable in the upper classes. We should be competing and winning in education and business instead, every other ethnic group, including some poor Whites, are flat out beating us. Even when we have the money to send our kids to the most elite private schools our kids' performance is still dead last.

Acting Black

Doctors Abigail and Stephen Thernstrom (2003), conservative researchers, state that race, more than money or any other factor, contributes to the underperformance of Black children. In their book *No Excuses: Closing the Racial and Learning Gap*, (2003) they surmise that the phenomenon of 'acting Black' is at the core of Black students' poor academic performance and by extension is what limits Black economic progress. They quote a National Education Longitudinal Study that found our students' perception of working "as hard as they (could) almost every day in their classes," was significantly different from that of their White and Asian counterparts, (Thernstroms, p.145). Working as hard as they could for Black students meant studying 3.9 hours per week according to the Thernstroms. White students said that they studied 5.4 hours a week to achieve 'hard as they could' while Asian students reported 7.5 hours a week to achieve the same end.

The liberal education expert Dr. James P. Comer agrees with the Thernstroms as to what is central to academic and, by extension, professional success for Black people. In his book *Leave No Child Behind: Preparing today's youth for tomorrow's world* (2004), he too sees the need for our values to change. "The once powerful positive effects of well-functioning and/or church-based cultures have been decreased by the breakdown in community and the powerful effects of the mainstream media entertainment that glorifies often harmful nonmainstream habits and lifestyle," (Comer, p. 91). Acting Black has come to mean acting dumb.

The great philosopher James Allen wrote in *As a Man Thinketh* that, "As a being of Power, Intelligence, and Love and the lord of his own thoughts, man holds the key to every situation, and contains within himself that transforming and regenerative agency by which he may make himself what he wills," (Allen, p. 6). If we accept that Black and dumb are one, then that will become our view and we see all who look upon us the same. Allen tells us that what we think we are is who we are. Teaching our children the power of self-determination through preparation is not White any more than it is Black. This truth is universal and enduring, timeless and without question.

Money has not made us equal nor will it ever. Adopting a culture of success will save us from the ongoing impact of racism, both internal and external. Achievements and the extension of opportunities to others will transform the state of Black America. To make this real, the Black community must build a network of supportive people of all hues to thwart the impact of racism. This will improve our community and all of America.

Closing off the escape routes

In our desperate dash from the throes of racism we are all too happy to nestle into the thorny skin and unreliable embrace of a "good job." Somehow, like Native Americans selling Manhattan for $24, the Black middle class has signed a contract that convinced us that working in the same office signals equality. Our belief in the claim of equality from proximity has persuaded us to give away that which could sustain us. Malcolm X said in a 1961 speech at Harvard University that, "Integration is not good for either side," because he thought that the problems in the Black community would remain, (Epps, p. 127). Even though Malcolm and I disagree on this, it cannot be denied that the blind pursuit of integration devoid of a commitment to becoming self-sufficient has not led to a level playing field.

We have stopped depending on us and started trusting that someone else will take care of our community and its children. We have untied the boats of entrepreneurship that carried our community out of the most heinous bondage in the human experience. We have traded in our only hope for economic independence through entrepreneurship to drift on the shaky dinghy of a good job.

> "It is unfortunate, too, that the educated Negro does not
> understand or is willing to start small enterprises which make
> the larger ones possible. If he cannot proceed according to
> the methods of the gigantic corporations about which he
> reads in books, he does not know how to take hold of
> things and organize the communities of the poor along lines
> of small business, (Woodson, p. 48)."

We have to ask ourselves why don't more people in our
community live in a motel that we own or join our family to split 24
hour shifts at a 7 Eleven like the Patels do? Why don't we enter the
economy by way of owning a business that cleans offices at midnight
like the Rodriguezes do? "The Negro, from the point of view of
commerce and industry shows no mental power to understand the
situation which he finds," (Woodson, p. 48). Dr. Woodson is more
hard core than I am. I will say that we have gotten caught up in the
attractive, yet insecure position of an employee.

Dr. Woodson knew that foreigners understood the
circumstances surrounding the American economic experience better
than African Americans. He told us that our ignorance leaves the
field of industry wide open to people from other lands. "Foreigners
see (the opportunity to own business) as soon as they reach our
shores and begin to manufacture and sell to Negroes," (Woodson,
parenthesis added, p. 48). In 1933 they sold us clothes and today
they continue to satisfy our fix to look rich even when we are barely
making it. They sell us bags of hair, gold and nails. You name it,
immigrants have gotten our habits down. I dare you to try and find a
Black community whose commerce is not controlled by people with
a limited understanding of English but a vast understanding of the

91

opportunities that exist in this country for those willing to work hard.

The result of our pursuit of a good job and acceptance instead of ownership is that we are not invited to the American economic or political tables. Instead we are relegated to the consumer's kiddy table to watch "Sports Center" and look for a sale on shiny things. You name it and if it's shiny, we love it. Teeth, furs, rims, CD's, jewelry, cars, even our tires have to be shiny.

A Dr.'s note

At every point in the economic ladder and in every sector of the Great Experiment, African Americans are losing. Being Black doesn't mean being inferior. Accepting second class status does. Look at Black immigrants, then you will see how profound the African American experience is.

African, Afro-Caribbean and Black Latino students are entering the nation's top colleges at rates that are significantly higher than their piece of the population pie. They have rumbled their way through our schools and are now kicking Black American butts out of the seats of the Ivy Leagues. Then they are filling them with their sun kissed sub Saharan fire to live every minute of the American Dream regardless of their color. They have not bought into the distinctly American notion that some people are just born with it.

Our African, Afro-Caribbean and Black Latino brothers and sisters understand that the sweetest fruit does not fall to the ground, instead it requires its suitors to climb atop the shaky ladder of life to cajole its ample and succulent curves free. While immigrants of every single shade are training their children to be professionals, our kids are caught up in dreaming of becoming rappers and professional athletes. While their kids are studying twice as many hours per day, our boys are watching twice as much television.

The talented tenth is letting us down. It doesn't matter if they are in Black fraternities or sororities, professional or civil rights organizations or if they are unaffiliated members of the middle-class. Too many of us cannot free ourselves from the seduction of status. Instead of leading, we focus on being accepted, avoiding making waves and taking what we have been given:

> "Here we find that the Negro has failed to recover from his slavish habit of berating his own and worshiping others as perfect beings… The race is looking to this educated class for a solution to its problems and does not find a remedy, on the contrary, it sees itself further and further away from those things to which it has aspired," (Woodson, p. 109).

Who but a world-renowned brilliant Black professor would feel the need to justify himself to an institution that clearly said that it didn't want him? Especially when his own community would give an arm to have him back at one of their college's.

Paging Dr. West. …. Dr. Cornell West please put down your quest for acceptance and chill with your attempts at producing middle-aged Hip Hop. Please stop, you're embarrassing us.

You did a great job acting in the "Matrix Reloaded," now get out of your trailer and come to the front lines. Say something controversial and do something revolutionary like teaching at a Black college all year, instead of giving a two-hour $15,000 lecture there. We get it; you can work at Harvard University and teach the world's wealthiest children. Consider us very impressed. If you get a minute, can we bother you to build from the bottom brotha'? Don't write and talk about it, be about it. There are enough Black entertainers. Loosen the black scarf, we've got work to do. You are too brilliant to focus on the easy to hit targets. Leave those to the rest of us.

Society? C'mon you can do better than that. Leave that stuff to novices like me. We need you to lay some old fashion solutions on us. Talk about how the SAT is so racist that even backward California officials were going to stop using it. Lace us with some funky rifts on how successfully programs such as Upward Bound have served the poor for years. See, society, history, racism, classism are big concepts. We need policies.

Dr. Cornell West stands as an example of the middle-class paradox. We rest comfortably on the backs of a revolution, only to fall asleep. He, like so many of us, built a name by speaking about the revolution and the revolutionaries. Yet it is unclear what is revolutionary about his going from Harvard to Princeton. It's prestigious, but otherwise pretty predictable. Hampton University must not have been hiring Sociology professors. No community college students needed access to the richness of his research on Mondays and Wednesdays from 8:30 to 9:50 a.m. either. It's a good thing he stayed put. The 100 or so highly motivated, mostly West Indian or African Black students and their too liberal for words White friends, would have been lost without him.

A man of half his wealth and influence could breathe life into one of the nearly dead historically Black colleges that dot our Southern belly. The sheer magnitude of such a move could inspire the likes of Dr. Henry Louis Gates of Harvard University to leave the crisp comfort of Cambridge, MA for the dry heat of a Southern Black college campus.

Tragically he, Dr. Gates, and the rest of the eloquent historians, like so many in the middle-class, will not give up their seat in the Big House. They appear afraid. Of what, only God knows.

One answer is clear, we like shiny things. So, a caution to Dr. West et al, don't be fooled by the shine of the Ivy. It's prestigious and poisonous when you consume it. Let the status thing go! Please. We really need you down here on the coliseum floor.

The prescription for our success is to get as many so called civil rights leaders, thinkers and talent to the heart of the issues that plague our community. When the ordained leaders start to lead, the rest of the Black middle class will follow.

Glory days

Our community's so-called civil rights leaders and organizations should have seen this one coming. If you have been reading this book and you didn't think your turn was on its way, then I am not surprised. This is the problem, you have been watching from the sidelines too long. You are not a spectator. You are our civil rights team. You're wearing that uniform for a reason. There's a civil rights struggle under way. At some point you had to realize that somebody is gonna expect you to be a player in the struggle.

Come on out, it's time to talk. Civil rights organizations were formed to come up with answers that will save our community from eminent ruin. Unfortunately, civil rights leaders have been entangled in the easy prey and one-sided skirmishes of White racism, gangster rap and Republicans. In the meantime the rest of the culprits of Black destruction loot our community without as much as a whimper from the leaders in civil rights.

Instead of calling out enemies to Black progress, which would include at times the organization itself, the major civil rights organizations have taken to crafting excuses for why Black people are in what often feels like a petrified state of failure. These cats have more excuses than a child holding a broken vase staring down the barrel of a switch. Simply put, if Black civil rights organizations' leaders were fulfilling their responsibility to lead us out of the doldrums of our present, then there would be no way that we would have become more immersed in it over the past 50 years.

Civil rights organizations like the National Association for the Advancement of Colored People and the National Urban League are making a killing off of poverty. Once upon a time they guided us through the storms of insidious racism for nothing more than travel expenses, a fish sandwich and hot sauce. Today, careers and courses of study have been built on the backs of the leaders who framed the struggles of inclusion and wrestled the knots of Jim Crow loose so that we could send our children to integrated schools, come down out of the balconies of movie theaters, and if we chose, or even marry a White woman.

We are 50 years and counting past the civil rights movement. "Oratory and resolutions do not avail much," Dr. Woodson warned 20 years prior to the civil rights movement. "If they did," he said, "the Negro race would be in a paradise on earth, (p. 118)." He told us that, "old men talk of what they have done, young men talk of what they are doing, and fools of what they expect to do. The Negro race," he concluded, "has a rather large share of the last mentioned class," (p. 118).

The days of slow walking and hymn singing need to be treated like a thin spry James Brown. Both are pleasant memories, but that is all that they are. Brown is heavy and confirmed crazy and we need to put some pep in our step, then change what is coming out of our mouths.

We don't need to fight fights that we have already won. This is like a fat woman in a thong. Good idea but it is poorly placed. Thousands of patriots of all hues fought against segregation. What is left is a more insidious, de facto segregation. This is the segregation that ensures that almost no Black males entering their freshman year in high school will be enrolled in algebra. Combating issues like this is how true civil rights soldiers earn their stripes. Leaders of the past have left us with the responsibility of changing the culture that allows apartheid to take shape in the U.S. The bygone soldiers won the first phase of the war by kicking the doors out of squalor off their hinges. Fifty years ago they made it illegal to kill Black boys. Today we are still celebrating in the streets as our boys kill each other at rates that make lynching look like the flu. There is still much work to be done so put down the champagne and get back to work.

The civil rights movement did not erase the hate that racism fostered, only the most obvious policies. It also did not erase White racism's two bastard children, Black on Black racism and White moderates. Both of these accept that being Black means being less than. This means less capable and willing to live out our true abilities, push our talents and inspire a new generation. These issues are the roots of Black on Black violence and teachers who give up on our kids before ever giving them a chance. Our past civil rights leaders fought and won the first round. The bell is sounding on us now.

Today's civil rights organizations look like old fat men talking about high school football games. These 50-year-old victories no longer validate the present purpose of the leaders or their organization. It is a new day with new challenges. We cannot organize against the enemy outside of the community when the most dangerous are within. We cannot use old tactics to fight the new logic of integrated schools with segregated classrooms, teachers' unions that sign contracts allowing them to stay after school for only ten minutes or the new "Colored Only" signs known as corporate glass ceilings.

New paradigms need to be adopted to confront under-education that leads to under employment, unemployment and a life of incarceration. If the civil rights organizations were still fighting they would not allow even Black teachers to consistently provide any child with an education that is so bad that the teachers refuse to give it to their own kids. These are the fights that lay ahead. Take off your letterman's sweater, put away you dashiki, get a haircut and get ready to earn the position that your education and our ancestors paid for.

Lost symbolism

The "Eyes on the Prize" series, Black History Month, Martin Luther King, Jr.'s holiday, schools and streets, and the commercial acceptance of Kwanzaa could possibly be some of the most detrimental symbolic victories since the civil rights movement. Together they give Black people pause for reflection, celebration and acceptance annually without ever having to do another thing amidst one of the community's darkest hours.

Even raggedy schools can make sense of the "Eyes on the Prize" series. The most racist company can acknowledge Black History Month. Dr. Martin Luther King, Jr.'s birhday is a national holiday. The streets and schools named in his honor are either in the worst parts of town or obscure side streets. The sentiment is lost there too. Hallmark has co-opted Kwanzaa and through the likes of Reverend T. D. Jakes' line of greeting cards makes it is as easy to celebrate as Easter. All of these symbols were once representations of unmitigated defiance. Today they droop like an old red, black and green flag whose colors we don't understand. The buses are full of Black people from the driver to the back. The lunch counters are closed. Even Denny's says that they want your business back.

Overrated and unorganized

African Americans have formed professional organizations based upon a shared culture and training. Organizations like the National Black MBA's (NBMBA), National Association of Black Journalists (NABJ), social workers, engineers, lawyers, doctors, nurses, etcetera each act as both a source of inspiration and frustration for the Black community. Each organization boasts members that are highly educated professionals, who are capable and upwardly mobile.

With all the talent that our professional groups purport to possess, the African American community should be doing pretty well. Unfortunately, these groups, the community at-large, have not arrested control of even a small portion of our power. In affect, we are gladly giving our money and the education of our children away to other communities in exchange for some of their shiny things.

All of our professional organizations will do more good than harm. All have a very valid purpose and should remain in tact. Each could improve the practice of its members and give them more opportunities for jobs. What they need to do though is to become deft at organizing their members' resources in a meaningful manner so as to harness our community's great potential.

At this moment, then, the Negroes must begin to do the very thing that which they have been taught that they cannot do…They must begin immediately to pool their earnings and organize industries to participate in supplying social and economic demands. If the Negroes are to remain forever removed from the producing atmosphere, and the present discrimination continues, there will be nothing left for them to do, (Woodson, p.108).

Black professional organizations are comfortably marginalized by the power brokers and painfully distant from the comprehensive fundamental needs of the community. Most Black professional organizations focus on their members' need to get good jobs instead of building opportunity. It shows.

While these groups' members may keep a good job the Black community posts the highest unemployment in the nation. According to Census data, 11.3% of Black men spent 2004 without a job. That number is projected to increase to 12.2% in 2005. By comparison our unemployment rates are almost twice that of all other men from any ethnic group; Asian, 4.2%, White, 5.4%, and Latino 6.4%.

The NBMBA's claim to have 40 chapters throughout the United States. The mission listed on their official website is to lead "in the creation of intellectual and economic wealth of the African-American community," (ww.nbmbaa.org). From this statement one could believe that NBMBA builds community banks and socially conscience corporations while teaching others how to do the same. In actuality, not so much.

Anecdotal examples of individual members doing great things cannot be taken as the deeds of the organization any more than similar examples of NBMBA's members who have broken the law. Their mission must be fully realized. Its collective efforts must be visible through clear and present organized large scale acts that extend beyond hooking a frat brother up with a good job at Chase Manhattan, where neither one of them end up having any juice.

This association claims that their members are "thousands of the brightest and most determined graduate students and experienced professionals to be found anywhere." Combining this groups members resources to do something as simple as buying property should be easy, right? Good luck finding just one of the 40 chapters that have done so. It is not clear if any of the chapters even own a washtub to store ice. It would be interesting to see how many chapters of "the brightest and most determined graduate students and experienced professionals to be found anywhere" have settled for collectively owning nothing more than some NBMBA letterhead.

The NBMBA's don't run a single business. There are local Black churches that have millions in land and other holdings. These same groups run credit unions that offer low interst loans to the community and or their members for homes, buisnesses and college. Yet the NBMBA has not combined their talent and resources to establish much-needed business in blighted Black communities. Not even a franchise. Not a single fried chicken chain, rib shack or corner liquor store, but they sure can throw a conference. With the precision of a laser they can secure a block of rooms in a White owned hotel and party 'til the break of dawn.

The NBMBA may retort that collectively owning businesses is not their purpose, which would spark a question, "What did you mean when you stated that your organization sought to create intellectual and economic wealth for the African American community?"

Ownership is how wealth is built. MBA's of every color

know this. This is a basic concept that has galvanized and insulated other communities. You cannot pass down a job, but wealth can grow and live forever. Too much of the Black middle class is selling the flawed logic that says that when we have a good job its effects trickle down on the rest of the community. Trickle down economics didn't work for Ronald Reagan and it hasn't worked for the Black community either. Collective responsibility, my brothas, ownership and collective responsibility, are what we need to grow.

If we in the Black professional organizations cannot pool resources together for our greater good, who will? Woodson said that we, "must begin immediately to pool (our) earnings and organize industries to participate in supplying social and economic demands," (Woodson, p. 108, parenthesis added). He concluded by saying that if we don't put our resources together then we would, "forever be removed from the producing atmosphere, and the present discrimination continues, there will be nothing left for the Negroes to do," (Woodson, p. 108).

Another powerful and well-positioned professional African-American organization is the 30 year old National Association of Black Journalists, NABJ. This organization represents almost every single African-American in the media.

What is the name of NABJ's newspaper, publishing company, television and radio stations? You don't know either? NABJ's members work for the world's largest media outlets, yet when they come together as a group, the result is another swanky conference. Sure high schoolers all over the world can and do publish newspapers, as well as produce TV and radioshows. Of course NABJ's members have the ability to create publishing and broacast outlets, but they don't!

Enough already with the conferences. Combine your talents to build small local Black newspapers or radio stations. Organize to do something other than hold a week long meeting to talk about how tough it is to be Black and in the media. Do something to change our condition by changing your own. It is impossible for the rest of us to feel sorry for intelligent people who have the ability to improve their condition.

What if NABJ could have come together to have saved amazing magazines like Emerge? What if great magazines like Black Enterprise were joined by equally well thought out lifestyle periodicals run by the NABJ? Who needs Simon and Schuster to push our books when we have an organization full of media savvy Black people who have spent decades infiltrating our communities on behalf of White publishing goliaths? What if NABJ used what they have learned to tell our story the way we want it told? Everyone from authors to the audience needs you to do what you were trained to do, but this time we need you to do it for our community. Hell, I could have used you to put this and my other two books out. In fact, there are thousands like me who need what you know to move the community forward or at least to start a discussion.

Think of the impact that this organization's reported 3,300 members could make if they organized their collective gifts and created a national Black wire service from which the news could be accessed in Anytown, USA. We would be carrying forward the traditions of drummers and griots with the exactitude and range of modern technology. Then small local presses would have immediate national appeal with local roots. Local writers could take hold of a national audience by telling their community's story to all of us . This would transform the world's image of Black people.

Think, if you will of this, when was the last time that you saw a Black person represented in a mainstream newspaper above the fold who was doing well? If you are Black and on the front page of a mainstream newspaper, then you can kiss your career and ass goodbye. Conversely, when have you seen a Black owned publication portray a Black person negatively? The Black press is so kind to Black people that not even the D.C. Sniper was scorched.

How powerful the impact on the Black conscience and outlying communities would be if the NABJ's members did more than just report the news and began to make it? We might finally have more to dine on with in the evening than the endless Black boy perp' walks of entertainers and professional athletes. The Black experience is more than a police blotter or entertainment piece. No one knows that better than you, NABJ. You could tell the rest of the world real stories of extraordinary people of all colors. Isn't that why you signed up? Stop blaming your program directors and editors for misrepresenting our people. It's our story so we have to tell it.

When Lacey Peterson, the pregnant California woman, was reported missing, the mainstream media exploded with coverage. All major television networks and countless periodicals held a vigil until her dismembered remains washed ashore. When Latoyia Figueroa, a pregnant Philadelphia woman, was reported missing there was little more than a mainstream media pop.

The story lines were the same, young pregnant women missing, the colors were different. Strangely, some of us are surprised by the undeniable disparity in coverage and the implied value extended to the Black experience. These must be the same people who were shocked by the grotesque beating Rodney King received at the hands of those employed to protect and serve. This same nad've core expects somebody else to tell our story the way we think that it should be told. They haven't accepted the fact that Black villains, O.J., Michael Jackson, R. Kelly, Mike Tyson et al, sell mainstream media. Whereas Black victims from as far back as Emmett Till don't.

Conducting community affairs for your station ain't what we're talking about here. It's great that you spent a half hour at a middle school last week, I did too. What we need is for organizations like NABJ to leverage their resources and talent in more meaningful ways. Look, fundamentally impacting the African-American condition through words and images means just that, fundamentally impacting things. Create a dialogue around issues such as modern racism, internal and external, discuss solutions and then burn them into the world's conscious with your mighty roaring pens.

NABJ may also argue that they are a professional organization that exists to get and keep jobs for their members. This too begs a question, "If NABJ helped keep someone other than Radio One and Black Entertainment Television in business, wouldn't this create more jobs for NABJ members?"

If organizing the members for something other than a conference is too much, then start with something as simple as listing the names of Black owned newspapers and radio stations on the NABJ website. Maybe even include a link to their top stories. Another small place to start is by taking a percentage of membership dues and using it to purchase a yearly subscription to a local or national Black owned press, magazine or whatever. Consider it media tithing. How much is an annual newspaper subscription, $50?

Let the members choose which publication they'd like to send the percent of their dues to, but make the choice count by keeping our stories coming, which means keeping the Black press alive.

The National Association of Black Social Workers (NABSW) has a code of ethics that speaks to me, but I'm a Black social worker, so it should.

> If a sense of community awareness is a precondition to humanitarian acts, then we as Black Social Workers must use our knowledge of the Black community, our commitment to its self-determination, and our helping skills for the benefit of Black people as we marshal our expertise to improve the quality of life of Black people, (www.nabsw.org, Code of Ethics).

Position papers and conferences in sexy locales don't spell solution, even if you are a social worker.

Where are NABSW run treatment centers, homeless shelters, schools and summer food service programs? These were programs independently managed with amazing efficiency and limited resources by the Black Panthers in the early 1970's. What's stopping modern social workers from doing the same? National Black Social Workers are no different than our equally well-educated professional brethren. We want good jobs.

If we are who we claim to be, then Black social workers do not need anybody to take the primary responsibility of mending our community. Of course we want, need and should have global support. It is foolish to think that Black people from any profession can fix, by themselves, what racism and classism have brought upon us. But we need to lead the way.

The way NABSW's Code of Ethics declares our

professional commitment to self-determination and utilizes our helping skills motivates me. I became a social worker to marshal our expertise to improve the quality of life of Black, Latino and poor White people. Feeling committed is a nice place to start, but just like our MBA friends, we need to do more than talk about self-determination.

The same applies to Black nurses and doctors' professional organizations. They don't have a hospital, clinic or an outhouse where they can come together to find a cure for something as basic as shaving bumps. National Black Engineers, you build stuff, really big stuff. Do you have even as much as a designated tree house within which you can hold local meetings? Lawyers, can you help us deal with racist sentencing, treasonous teachers unions that are strangling our children's futures or lenders who think that being Black equals having bad credit?

A token of appreciation

Black people give at a higher rate than any other group according to a 2005 online survey in *Black Enterprise*. When we give though, our gifts are not well planned and splintered, thus we find ourselves spitting in the ocean to try to change the direction of the current, instead of learning to master the waves. Our well-intentioned disjointed gifts need to be traded in for meaningful contributions that transform the conditions under which we live. Therefore, if we give to a church, let that be a church with a credit union that offers low-interest rate loans. Let's relax for a minute on the pastor's anniversary, he had a big enough one last year.

Black professionals with more education than necessary to know better, annually pile into somebody's loaned or rented space to plan unambitious scholarship fundraisers. The booty from the event that took exactly one year of planning can range from $500 to $10,000. This then means that five lucky kids will each get a $500 one-time book scholarship. Nationally, the rewards increase, but not the impact or numbers served.

The national chapters of the Black MBA's and Black Journalists combined in 2005 to grant scholarships a total of 35 children scholarships. There are 34 million African Americans, most of whom are kids. Thirty-five scholarships from two of the nation's largest Black professional organizations are unacceptable.

What is most disappointing about these well-intentioned but poorly planned gestures is that the overwhelming majority of individual members could give $500 to a kid by themselves. It borders on ludicrous that together local and national professional Black organizations only come up with enough money for a few kids to buy a few books for one damn semester. Then we lament over the low rate of Blacks graduating from college.

Yeah yeah, if you add up all of the $500 local or $5,000 national scholarships they'd equal... who knows what they'd equal and who cares? What they do not equal is fundamental change. What these gifts will not have produced is the commitment necessary to extinguish the wall of flames that engulf our kids and us. Don't break your arms patting yourselves on the back. We might need you to use them to shake yourself into being honest.

Our community's problems are bigger than scholarships and Black professionals know it. Stop throwing nickels at a million dollar problem. One year in an East Coast private college can cost over $42,500. One year of locking a child up in a juvenile justice facility in the same region costs the taxpayers over $500,000 and 50% of these kids will end up back in jail. One $400 scholarship from a group of people whose median income is at least $60,000 a year speaks to the middle-class' absolute disconnection from the people we left behind.

When the suit you wore to the last scholarship gala was worth more than the scholarships, you know that it is time to cancel the ceremony next year. Invite the kids to your house and just give them the check. Imagine how much more money you could award and how much more the gift of inviting the child into your home would mean to the child and community.

"Negroes often find themselves giving money and moral support to various institutions and causes which influence the course of the race the wrong way," (Woodson, p. 117). Using the example of a preacher driving up in a Cadillac, Dr. Woodson said that we should see that a preacher who does this, "does not come to feed the multitude spiritually. He comes to fleece the flock," (p. 124). He said that we don't ask ourselves if the support that we are giving will, "rebound in the long run to the good of the people," (p. 118). Dr. Woodson concluded by saying that we don't inquire whether the assistance that we are providing, "offers temporary relief but eventually results in irreparable loss," (p. 118).

Pied Pipers

We have established that many of today's rappers say and do ignorant and destructive things. As ignorant as they can be, and whoa they can be ignorant, the absence of the Black middle class often makes them look like they are the only ones reaching out to our kids.

Puffy, Jay-Z and Russell Simmons have done their personal and professional dirt by peddling negative, and at times, pornographic images. For this there is no applause. However, they are no different than Black Entertainment Television's founder and long-time CEO, Bob Johnson, who gives them the vehicle for hours of soft porn, which he starts at 2:00 PM, just in time for the kids when they get home from school. This is the same Bob Johnson who proclaimed at the 2004 BET awards, among the likes of Snoop and reputed pimp, Bishop Magic Don Juan, that 'he' was the biggest pimp in the room. We know Bob. We know. All of these men fill a void that we have created.

Rappers like Master P, members of the Cash Money Click, Murder, Inc., Roc-a-Fella, Wu Tang Clan and even the infamous Suge Knight, are the ones showing poor kids how to own a business and build an industry. As misguided as their images are, the message cannot be lost that these men of little, and in some cases, no formal education have found a way to legally provide a blueprint for self sufficiency. While the MBA's and social workers talk about it, these men got it done. While the Black professional organizations' members are at a conference trying to get laid, they are on the grind, trying to change the world.

Say what you want about their music but the message that many of the kids get is that somebody has got to 'stick it to the Man' and we look like we are in bed servicing him. To our kids' untrained eyes these men stand as the truest examples of success to our children because the kids feel that these men have gone on and have not left them in the land of misfit toys.

Rappers exalt the challenges of poverty to a poetic, painful and compelling process. Rappers give the kids the feeling that they have moved up, but not on. These Hip Hop moguls make our kids feel that there is hope somewhere for people like them. Imagine how many more kids will make it out when more professionals reach back to bread the roads out of the despair of poverty, countering the notion that entertainment is the only way out.

These same amazingly successful, overly tattooed hood rats have done what the middle-class is afraid to do. They start businesses and change the world. While education has indebted so many of us in the middle-class to ungrateful corporations, brothas from the hood experience the winds of independence. Sure they will piss it all away on shiny things, but at least they can say that they tried.

To whom much is given, much is expected

The message that appears to be lost on our Black professionals and our civil rights organizations is that the world is watching. "The Negro must now do for himself or die out as the world undergoes readjustment," (Woodson, p. 107). Kids and adults of all colors want to see what we do with our time and talent. Then they will decide what they want to do to help or hurt the cause. When we seem self-centered, disorganized and unwilling to speak out, then they take our cue. They are silent and ineffective too.

"The program for uplift of the Negro in this country must be based upon a scientific study of the Negro from within to develop in him the power to do for himself what his oppressors will never do to elevate him to the level of others," (Woodson, p. 114). Our community's kids see us as all as what they hope to become. We must model in every stride that we take the commitment to learn to do for self. Handouts are recalls waiting to happen.

The educated amongst us represent the end point, the goal of a good life. We, more than any 19-year-old athlete or entertainer, inspire our community to go to school, say their prayers and eat their vegetables. We are the reason for sacrifice. It was in anticipation of our college graduation that somebody loved us enough to take out a switch, give us a curfew and dare us to dream beyond the unreasonable limitations of racism. Let's let our communities know that we appreciate their trust and understand our role.

"The race will free itself as soon as it decides to. No one else can accomplish this task for the race. It must plan and do for itself," (Woodson, p. 117). I am extremely proud to point out that we have the tools. Our Black professional and civil rights organizations have led the way in the creation of infrastructures that could give rise to opportunities untold. Our community is fortunate to have in place, the structures we lack, only to have the strategies to move us out of the doldrums of our current condition.

We, especially those of us who have the means to do something about it, must truly start to believe and then invest in us. The Black community needs to practice affirmative action within its own community. "Negro banks, as a rule, have failed because the people, taught that their own pioneers in business cannot function in this sphere," (Woodson, p. 108). We have to give our vendors as fair a shot as we do others.

Dr. Woodson's most revelatory assertion was that we should abandon the leadership model for one of service. He felt that it is up to all of us to grab hold of our responsibilities. In his notion of community empowerment, the community was truly empowered. There was no time to wait for someone else to save us. Salvation is ours.

In those days one could have argued that our community was barely out of legalized slavery. In 1933 Woodson was speaking to a segregated and ostracized group. Who would he be speaking to today?

Then, as is the case now, the Black community needed the Black middle class to organize in order to create opportunity. We have organized and opportunity has been created. Only a fool would argue that things are just as they were in the early 20th century. Though a thoughtful person could see significant similarities and would question what often feels like scant gains.

No community is without its challenges, but the Black community will always have to contend with racism. We will forever have to convince ourselves and others that we are as good and skin is just that, skin. It does not color our capacity.

Our professional and civil rights organizations can open businesses and schools, create media opportunities that will both employ and educate, counsel and cure those issues that are distinctly culturally ours and legislate against the hateful tendencies of a nation that, like Germany, has a past that they'd rather not discuss.

Collective responsibility can improve our community. It is not an esoteric dream. We have established the organizations, we now just need to respond to the changing needs and times. Black professional and civil rights organizations must redefine the focus. As long as there is racism we will need to ensure that laws and hiring do not go against us, but that front of the struggle is well in hand. Internally we are most in need of action.

While we fought to be accepted into the White community's buses, businesses and schools, we let our own go to hell. When was the last time that you saw a Black owned pharmacy? Essential elements of our community exist only in grayed and torn photographs.

The Black middle class has the capacity and structures to improve our community. The question is, will it?

Pulpit Pimpin':
Birmingham is on
Fire
Chapter 5

Pulpit Pimpin': Birmingham is on fire

The Black community is being decimated and our Black preachers are preoccupied with growing their own churches and flushing out homosexuals. While the community burns to the ground the Black pulpit has been reduced to commentators, talkers, with thin words and empty promises.

These once proud cadres of Christian revolutionaries have become relics. "The church was very powerful in the time when the early Christians rejoiced at being deemed worthy to suffer for what they believed," Dr. King wrote as he lamented in a 1963 Birmingham jail. Dr. King was nine years into the thankless pursuit of justice that eventually cost him his life.

The truth is that Dr. Martin Luther King, Jr. probably would not have been invited to many of today's sterilized Dr. King celebrations. These typically pointless gatherings would have served as an opportunity for the warrior of peace to blast a gaping hole in the audience's day. He would have rumbled with his typically righteous indignation for the lack of progress that the community and country are making towards genuine equality. Dr. King was the real deal, a serious threat to the status quo. He had balls to take on that generation's biggest threats. That's why they killed him. Many of his contemporaries survived the civil rights movement with little more than a scratch and a trunk full of stories.

Dr. King has left us with poignant words and deeds that should stand as a blueprint for how real preachers should lead. He had little patience for the shuckin' and jivin' Negroes of his day. He saw them as being integral to the problems that he was fighting. Sure, he had a problem with White leaders, but he also had problems with the Black ones too, especially those within the church.

We need only look at what he said in his *Letter from a Brimingham Jail* to find that Dr. King expected more of the church's leadership. He is said to have written this as he sat in prison once again forfeiting the company of his family and the comfort of a middle class intellectual. No matter where he wrote it, it is clear that he was both outraged and disappointed.

Once again he was shackled to his calling and chided by other clergy. Dr. King thought that it was a purpose of Christian leaders to empty their sanctuaries into the streets to save the lives of the oppressed and the souls of the oppressors.

In 2006, as was the case in 1963, the Black church is as

much a part of the solution as it was the problem. It is often said that we need another Dr. King. While this may be true, how would we respond to him were he here? We know how his contemporaries responded to him. Is Black America ready to look upon itself and its religious leaders as a major part of the problem? Dr. King did.

If we want another Dr. King, let us first take heed to the words of the one we had. To do this we can use the *Letter from a Brimingham Jail* to assess the success of the Black church's impact on the community.

Dr. King felt that the church's responsiveness to the community's needs has always been a means by which we could measure our progress towards self-sufficiency and equality. He reminded us that, "In those days (of early Christianity) the church was not merely a thermometer that recorded the ideas and principles of popular opinion; it was a thermostat that transformed the mores of society," (King, parenthesis inserted).

In the *Letter from a Birmingham Jail* Dr. King wrote that he " must honestly reiterate that I have been disappointed with the church. I do not say this as one of those negative critics who can always find something wrong with the church. I say this as a minister of the gospel, who loves the church; who was nurtured in its bosom; who has been sustained by its spiritual blessings and who will remain true to it as long as the cord of Rio shall lengthen." The fuel for Dr. King's disappointment was a church that was woefully neglectful of its responsibility to beat back oppression wherever it appeared. It is hard to believe that if Dr. King were living today that he would feel any differently. The condition of Black people has changed from 1963, but it is not significantly better. As stated many times throughout this book, African Americans are last in most reasonable measures of quality of life. This was the case in 1963 and remains so in 2006.

Dr. King could just as easily have been preaching last Sunday when he said that, "Things are different now. So often the contemporary church is a weak, ineffectual voice with an uncertain sound. So often it is an arch defender of the status quo. Far from being disturbed by the presence of the church, the power structure of the average community is consoled by the church's silent and often even vocal sanction of things as they are." Today's status quo equals bullets flying past our children's ears in our neighborhoods on their way to schools that resemble 1950's segregated failures. We need the Black church to organize its many houses of worship to break the status quo and save our community.

The leaders of the Black church must call to the carpet our self-destructive habits and the public policies that support them. Our church is yet another Black organization that has the authority, power, position and responsibility to at least question our current status. There is no reasonable explanation as to why organizations such as this shouldn't be able to transform the condition in their communities. One theory is that the Black church has been co-opted by political interests, divisiveness, petty personality conflicts, simple-minded attacks on homosexuals and visionless opportunists.

The table is set for justice

The United States is a nation politically structured to accommodate change, unrest, and if necessary, straight up drama. The Black community has had to test the buoyancy of this nation, its laws and moral its foundation. Black religious leaders have traditionally led the assault on injustice, internal neglect and external responsibility.

History screams that it was the Black pulpit that demanded freedom from slavery and segregation, and sought a governmental foundation for equality. There has always been a small group of preachers of varied educational levels who were singularly driven by a consistent passion to uplift the entire community and change the world one small town at a time. These men of peace waged war on racism and through the 1960's they were winning. Black religious leaders were victorious because, as Dr. King said, his "hopes had been blasted, and the shadow of deep disappointment settled upon (activists. They) had no alternative except to prepare for direct action, whereby (they) would present (their) very bodies as a means of laying our case before the conscience of the local and the national community," (King).

Black preachers, where ya' at, make some noise

The church is not above reproach nor are its leaders, not now or eva'. This is not a "slap your preacher" movement. It is an altar call. It is an honest to goodness look at the Black church's effectiveness in providing a parachute for the downward spiral of the Black community.

The Black church is the single largest organization in both size and influence in the Black community. The overwhelmingly Black National Baptist Convention USA Incorporated alone boasts eight million plus members. The Black church has a hold on our hearts that is unmatched. Every Black person has or will spend time in a Black church. It is an institution that is unavoidable. This scope of influence positions Black religious leaders to touch the hearts and minds of us all.

Dr. King was one of the great Black religious leaders. Now, there are more. The Black church is more than just another Black institution that should and could improve the state of Black America. It's bigger than that. The Black church is the single most powerful institution in the Black community that has ever existed. It is also the single largest Black run entity in the world, period. It, therefore, must claim a proportionate level of responsibility for the current state of Black America.

In a Jewish community there is likely one synagogue and countless Jewish owned businesses. In the Black community there are countless churches with almost no Black owned businesses. The disproportiante number of Black churches to synagogues is another example of the splintering of our resources.

Black people contribute to Black churches, well…umm, religiously. Even if we don't buy a single Black owned product, shop at a Black owned grocery store, or buy a single Black publication all week, our Black owned and operated churches will get their 15% of our wages by Sunday at 11:30 AM. The steady monetary support given every week by millions of Black people, rich and poor, to our churches is further evidence of the present power that our churches maintain.

We are born into, grow up in and, even after years of hiatus, will go home in a Black church. There is no organization that permeates more of our lives, minds and hearts than the Black church. Even Whites, Muslims and Jews know this. The world over knows that the Black pulpit is the center of the Black American universe. This is why every two-bit politician plods through any church that will have him in a bid to be elected. If a spiritually sound community is the mark of an effective Black church, then the Black church is the clearest example of a Black institution that has been rendered ineffective.

Blind faith is just that. We have trusted that our pastors have our best interests in mind. Is not the state of Black America a condition worth addressing?

By all accounts Black America is in trouble and we can't blame it all on racism, Hip Hop and public schools. We have allowed the church's leaders to convince us that symptoms such as gangster rap as the primary source of our demise instead of a result of a troubled community. No matter the rapper, none of them will ever have as much influence as the Black church. More Black people will sit in a Black church by the close of this week than will ever buy a gangsta' rap CD. More Black people will spend more years of their lives in churches than shaking their butts in a nightclub. The church and its leaders have been allowed to point the finger at everybody else while skipping itself.

Our faith in our religious leaders has made it too easy to transfer responsibility to popular culture and the police. The church is a mirror of society's need to scapegoat . It exemplifies our unwillingness to deal with the fundamental causes of fatherless communities and a lack of focus on our education.

At some point somebody has got to acknowledge that the Black church can and must fulfill its responsibility to inspire souls, organize skills and be the catalyst for our community's salvation. Over 40 years ago Dr. King warned that "if today's church does not recapture the sacrificial spirit of the early church, it will lose its authenticity, forfeit the loyalty of millions, and be dismissed as an irrelevant social club with no meaning for the twentieth century," (King). Well, it's the 21st Century y'all. The community needs direction and we can't hear you.

Bigger than God

The Black church is a behemoth and its leaders are about the same size. Black preachers are the most important Black public figures in the world. With that much influence they should be able to affect more positive change. They should be able to improve schools. Instead they focus on inconsequential rituals like putting prayer back in them. The kids know how to pray, it's reading, writing and arithmetic with which they are having problems.

Politics and the pulpit have always gone hand-in-hand. What were Mother Theresa and Pope John Paul II if not political activists? Poor people of all nationalities are dying because they don't have access to adequate health care. Church leaders could organize to impact this.

The political juice that the church earned in the civil rights movement has now gone stale. If the church was still respected like it was in the 60's, today there would be no way that affirmative action and federal student loan programs could be allowed to suffer from diminished resources, ineffective administration and uninspired delivery. These essential programs were born in the clergy-run civil rights movement and raised by our Black preachers.

Jesus led a movement to challenge the power structure to make a way for the meek to inherit the earth. Black preachers must take a cue from the Son of God or they will look like wayward bastard children. They must love the community like He loved the church.

Preacher or Pimp?

No one matters more to the flock than their Shepherd. These men, and few women, (the Black church is nothing if not sexist), bare a tremendous responsibility for the oft called moral decay of the Black community. As moral leaders there is no one else to assign the task of the Black community's moral salvation.

Men like me cannot be left home alone with the daunting task of improving the moral health of our community. We need help with our own moral shortcomings. So we should be given smaller jobs like cutting the church's lawn. We need spiritual leaders who take pride in their craft and foster their calling. Wretches like me need men and women in the pulpit to show us how to dodge the temptations of the world. We need preachers who have distinguished themselves from us by reminding us, through their deeds, that God has called them. Unfortunately though, too often our preachers are seduced by the same demons, like excess and ego, they are ordained to address.

Line up three egotistical Black preachers and three Black pimps, all in their Sunday bests. You'll see apple, grape and chartreuse, (okay maybe not chartreuse, but you get the picture) colored suits and shoes. Gold, platinum and diamonds will adorn their fingers, wrists, necks and teeth. Then look at the car that they drive. Whew! If it's not big, new and expensive they want nothing to do with it.

This small, colorful and very visible sect of the Black Christian leadership has commandeered the image of the Black preacher and church, and with it our people much like gangster rappers, have high jacked the image of the young Black man. These soulless snake oil salesmen have wiggled their way to the fore of our community and they are taking with them our community's dignity.

Preacher pimps are focused on increasing their bottom line but their efforts do not improve the status of anyone other than themselves. Which begs the question, "How much money does it take to run a church?"

Most churches have no more than 1.5 full-time employees, and one tax-free building with anywhere from 5 to 15,000 members paying weekly. Assistant ministers are there on a per diem basis. Guest preachers are pretty much the same. They get what they can collect at the end of the service. If the church has a school, there is tuition. Elderly housing, daycare services, are both delivered for a fee and or often supplemented by church members acting as volunteers. What then is the money from fundraisers, grants and planned giving going towards?

Every Sunday, billions are spent to free our souls while the band plays, the choir sings, fish is fried, cakes are baked, and pastor's anniversaries come and go. The building fund and special offering plates pass from lap to lap, snaking through the tight pews freed for a moment by white-gloved deaconesses, who then pile them atop one another right before they disappear into a room never again to be seen while the organist pounds. Cars are washed, fashion shows are sponsored, and liturgical dancers contort and twist to the sound of His Word as passions spew for a new day and $5 admission for kids and $15 for adults is collected at the door.

Penniless parishioners pray for prosperity, punching the air as the Holy Ghost sweeps them into a spinning frenzy accompanied by banging tambourines and hands clapped raw. The preacher pats his brow with a garishly white towel, squeezes a call for shared responsibility for the church's fiscal well being through burned out vocal cords predictably punctuated by a flaming organist. The sermon ends. Then the instruments plod on for a spiritual jam session. Gossip trickles and then pours to the cars filled with rambunctious kids and the grandmothers who are raising them. As the pastor exits, with his fruit colored suit, tie and matching shoes, he is gliding towards a beautifully appointed car. The band slows to a stop and the preacher takes with him the potential that that service held for his congregation to respond to the larger community's needs.

Churches have a moral obligation to improve the lives of the community, but too often they, and egotistical leaders lead to a splintered community that is limping through the grip of second class citizenship. Black churches and liquor stores pepper the hood, both promising to elevate. Too often consumers of both are left with a Sunday afternoon headache.

The proximity of appearance for some preachers and pimps should not come as a surprise. Many a preacher has gone the route of hell raiser on his way to the pulpit. Both egotistical preachers and pimps often share the same talents and leadership skills. If a man valued material things when he was of the world, his heart may be changed but his habits could have stayed the same. This does not diminish the power of either's calling. Only God knows what is in a man's heart. We just get exposed to his deeds.

What would Jesus do

What would Jesus do if His people were being banished to deplorable living conditions by internal and external foes? Would he use his position for personal gain? Would a man who washed the feet of his followers and died a torturous death, in the midst of the struggle for right, use his power to purchase and then wear a large platinum diamond encrusted cross, complimented by a diamond-stud earring? …A preacher with an earring… sometimes even I've gotta laugh.

We know what Jesus did. He put His life on the line for His Father and His people. He allowed His naked and ravaged body to be dragged through dirt streets like James Meredith connected to a Texas' racist's pickup truck. Then he allowed His fate and suffering to be compounded as He was strung up on a wooden cross like a gutted pig so that we do not have to suffer. He made the ultimate sacrifice. Now all His preachers have to do is help people get jobs, find decent housing, and raise their kids. Jesus was a radical of the highest order. All preachers have to do is lead.

Good preachers must stand up and lead

If you, the good pastors, who account for most of the men and women who are called, want to save some souls, start with the men dressed like circus clowns. There's a good chance that the man that you save might be a misguided pastor or a pimp; both are in need of a visit with Jesus or at least you.

Clothes don't make the man, but they do make those of us who follow them look like fools. Their outfits are not the problem. It's what they represent. If a man wears a police uniform, somebody just might ask him for help. Face it, people are judged by how they chose to decorate themselves. So don't dress like a Christmas tree if you want to be taken seriously.

No, all pastors don't dress and act like court jesters, but damn it, too many do. When a man looks like he is focused on himself it is hard to see him any other way. Jesus wasn't a snazzy dresser, but he got it done. We need the good preachers to help these men refocus on the cause. Teach your brothers about humility. The tens of thousands of preachers who have a consistent and mature calling are simply not doing enough to speak out against the conspicuous consumption of their brethren. Police thyself.

Good preachers, you know who the false prophets are. You may even be friends with them. They cannot be allowed to continue in their pursuits because, as Dr. King told the clergy in his *Letter*,' "Shallow understanding from people of good will is more frustrating than absolute misunderstanding from people of ill will. Lukewarm acceptance is much more bewildering than outright rejection."

Take these misguided clergymen shopping in your modest car and talk to them as Dr. King did in his *Letter from a Birmingham Jail*. Tell them, as Dr. King did, to cut this crap. Okay that's not exactly what he said. Maybe you should use different words too. You are a preacher, but you get the point.

Tell these men of ample talent that they look nuts and worse still, what they are doing is wrong. The misuse of their position is affecting us all. The most serious offense is not their sense of fashion. It is as it was when Dr. King looked out through prison bars for answers, acceptance of the status quo. This is a problem when the status quo hurts our community. The status quo that put Dr. King in jail and ultimately took his life proliferates when the pulpit's purpose is overrun by ego. Defenders of the status quo killed Dr. King and the civil rights movement. We can't bring Dr. King back but we can revive the notion of religious leader fighting for civil rights.

Good preachers cannot simply write off their responsibility to impart purpose on the brethren. They cannot phone in their disapproval because, "We are caught in an inescapable network of mutuality," Dr. King wrote, "Tied in a single garment of destiny. Whatever affects one directly, affects all indirectly." The credibility of all Black preachers is questioned every time one of the pulpit pimps is identified as one of you.

These visionless preachers are bringing you and us down. If it is true that without vision, the people will perish, then we have a pretty damn good idea why the Black community is caught up in this inferno. "We will have to repent in this generation," Dr, King told us 40 years ago, "not merely for the hateful words and actions of the bad people but for the appalling silence of the good people." Misguided clergy are not using their incredible power and influence to organize the community, but we knew that. The bigger problem is that good preachers are allowing individualism to be seen as more important to the community. During their silence, materialism has become a greater value than altruism and being our brothers' keeper now sits on a dusty shelf.

This here is not about clothes and cars. That would be too simple. Changing their garb and forcing them on public transportation won't change what is in pulpit pimps' hearts. The issue that needs to be addressed is leadership in both word and deed.

It's about responsibility to answer to and live by a higher authority. Be human, preacher. That is your challenge. Then aspire to be more than just human. Lead, preach and save. You are our human voice of His word whether you like it or not. A reason the church is so big is because we need leaders and you passionate, charismatic, articulate and, at times, brilliant men fit the bill. You chose this life. Now we need you to live it.

Leadership from the pews

Parishioners who spend year after year in church also have responsibility for the failure of the church to meet the needs of their community. We too have sponsored individualism and personal decadence of our pastors. Preachers are men, at their best and worst. They get erections, develop affections, their hair grays and they move their bowels. They, like the brotha' on the block, need our support and guidance too. To guide them we must live a life worth following as well.

Create a church that leads. Demand that our pastors be a leader in the entire community, not just in our building. Black preachers are among the best-trained and equipped to lead.

Let the pride that we have in our church not be tied to the prestige of its members. Let our church pride rain down from its ability to shape the lives of the community, get people off of drugs and work through tough marriages. Let community revival be the calling card of our church.

We have to be ambitious in both our faith and actions. Jesus wasn't seen as the Messiah because He saved a single life, once. He moved nations and brought empires to their knees. These are His works. What are ours?

Feeding the homeless, for instance, will put food in their belly but that will not reduce homelessness in the community. It will not even make the person eating the food less homeless. Fighting abuse through opening treatment centers will. Allying with other churches that house a certain expertise in this brand of salvation will end homelessness for that person and return a much-needed productive man to our community. We have to ensure that we work to find fundamental solutions.

Require our pastors to change lives community wide, not simply feeds habits. If 50% of the Black churches in any Black community banded together for just one year to address almost any issue in that community, that issue would cease to be a problem. To achieve this level of positive impact the focus of the flock would have to change from growing single churches, to improving the entire Black community.

Imagine, if you will, what would happen if just 50% of the churches in your Black community came together to teach every single child, Black, White and caramel to read at a proficient level. That means, members positioning themselves every week for one calendar year to work in some capacity to support literacy in our community. The church members could be the drivers, prepare snacks, and create tutoring schedules or host reading sessions in our living rooms. We could babysit the tutor's kids, copy materials, get pencils, coordinate with teachers on the progress of the kids or anything else that would be required to ease the process of moving people and coordinating talent. There is no formal training in education needed to achieve this end. No money either. We don't even need to know how to read ourselves. Our role could be one of support. We could be the pencil getter or babysitter. We don't even have to like kids to organize to get the kids in our town reading at a proficient level in one year.

The preachers of Anytown, USA could make this happen tonight. Without permission from the school district, local government, unions, even the parents, the biggest, Blackest most powerful entity in the world could end illiteracy in a town in one calendar year. The only thing that stands in the way is the same thing that has corroded the Black clergy and with it our community -EGO.

A tradition of community service

The truth is that Black churches still do many of the things that they used to do. They still support individuals in need, individually. Shelters, elderly housing, schools, after-school programs all still run out of a great many Black churches. In some cases these church administered services may be the only such activities that the community has.

Coordination is and always has been the only means of effectively reconfiguring our world. The churches are not separated by interest, the overwhelming majority want to do good work. They are separated by ambition and ego. Being the church that the mayor visits has become more important than hosting the most effective pre-school.

In 1954 Black churches and community groups came together in Montgomery, Alabama and 386 days later they exploded the rationale of segregation for the entire world. This little city walked, car pooled, and flat out organized their foes. Led by a 25-year-old Reverend Dr. Martin Luther King, Jr., mastermind by NAACP President, E.D. Nixon, supported by the Eastern Star and the 36,000 Black people who got it right. The conditions were far worse then than anything that we can conjure up today. Still, they began the end to legal segregation. Today all we would have to do is to teach kids to read. No one will get hurt. No lawns will light up with flaming crosses. No jobs will be lost. We are talking about simple, inexpensive yet priceless works. So will you come? Will you put that preacher ego away and come to Jesus just now? He will save you. He will save you, just now.

Leaders lead

The challenge of spiritual and moral leadership is not finding allies. It is accepting our detractors. Effective spiritual and moral leaders do not seek acclaim, stability or wealth. They exist to right wrongs. These leaders therefore are not burdened by the need to win friends or build consensus. In order for them to be effective they must accept those who they feel best represent what they oppose. Supporters are a fickle group. They move with the tide. Leaders are leaders because they follow their heart, not the crowd.

Organize. Lead. Follow.

Regular Black Men
Chapter 6

We need everybody to just do something

We need more regular Black men. These are men of simple courage who understand that there is a future and all of us play a role in shaping it. Athletics, entertainment, medicine, law, politics, entrepreneurship, trash collection and education, these are professions, simply jobs. They are in no way to be confused as values, character or the measure of a man. Regular Black men are found in every city and town, in all professions. They are single and married, young and old.

This is not a call for saints.

We need the flawed souls of Black men's humanity who struggle each day to add to our community. We are a community of the chipped and perfectly human, challenged by high hopes and shortcomings. There are none among us who stand out front as perfect. We are all equally capable and troubled.

We need the rumble of imperfect men's voices to ring out and decry an end to the insidious internal destruction that ravages our collective body. We need regular Black men to squash thugs, redirect delinquent fathers, lead the middle class, challenge the wealthy, remind the preachers to lead and the teachers to teach, right after we check ourselves.

We need resolute backs that have been pressed against the cold stonewalls of racism and classism to be peeled and pointed erect. We need the slumped shoulders of self-hatred to square to a self-love so profound that it cannot be denied. These men will cast aside excuses like wood shavings. These regular Black men will not accept the spread of AIDS, children having babies or parents who use ignorance as an out from their responsibilities.

We need once bigoted eyes to open to the complexity of our ongoing struggle to be Black, male dreamers. Color is an accident of birth. Courage is a life long pursuit. To be courageous is to see beyond Black and White, poor or rich. Courage arrives with maturity of mind, body and spirit. Regular men must be mature enough to acknowledge limits as they seek opportunities to expand them. These courageous men know that the last great school has not been built and therefore they are working to create new ones. These men love Hip Hop enough to reconfigure its passion towards a positive place. These men of valor have friends who they both follow and lead. These men understand that complacency is a dank cold place for the feeble of mind.

We need the minds of courageous men to open to new enemies, partners and solutions. These regular Black men can no longer be fooled into thinking that all Black people are for us and all other races are against us. These men know better. They have seen some good in all colors from all socioeconomic backgrounds. They have traversed the shaky planks that connect communities of all kinds. These men understand that we must root out negativity because ill will, not color, economics or place of origin is the only true mark of the opponent.

We need the basic sweet brown sugar of freedom to liberate a taste for every single body's responsibility to end the tradition of failure in our community. Being Black and ignorant are inconsistent in their minds. Quitting is failure so they refuse to give up.

We need Black men who are rich, middle, working class and poor, straight, gay and bi, light as your favorite White boy and dark as coal. No one can claim that they alone are truly Black. Simple internalized divisions do not fool regular Black men. They know that being Black is a condition of birth, not a choice. Being a man is an ongoing process that must not be derailed by simply attacking other men because they look or love differently. Internalized 'isms are more dangerous than any external hatreds. Regular Black men know this and have focused on correcting wrongs as they seek similarities.

We need answers and we cannot avoid the tough questions. Regular Black men have to ask themselves how our community got this way, followed by, what do we have to do to change it?

Making sure our house is in order

We cannot stick our heads in the sand and tell ghost stories about the racist boogeyman that is keeping Black men down. That's how they got us the first time. Riding through the night, dressed in bed linens, White racists played on our willingness to succumb to superstitions. They knew us well because they had help. Too many of our people have been willing to sell us out for their own personal gain.

Courageous Black men know that it is too pedestrian to point the finger at the likes of Armstrong Williams, Clarence Thomas, and Roy Ennis. These cats are proud to poke holes in our opportunities. It is easy to see that they are working diligently with those who oppose remedying the wrongs of generations of racism, inhuman educational settings and a justice system that is so lopsided that it should not ever be referred to as anything but penal. We know who they are. Focusing our efforts on these types of men has gotten us nowhere. Let them be.

It is more important for us to organize against Black on Black violence as if it were police on Black violence. Work to correct schools and school systems that consistently fail, especially when we are teachers in them. Think more deeply, look into our own families, communities and selves to find enemies and friends.

Selfishness ain't a republican trait any more than altruism is a democratic hallmark. Like my grandmother used to say, 'people is people.' Drug dealers, bad teachers, greedy businessmen, and deadbeat fathers, stand in the way of our progress. It matters not that they are our friends or the same color.

An enemy of the community is an enemy of the community, especially when that enemy is within. Think more deeply. Even our friends can be enemies of the state. If our friend beats his wife, we might be cool, but that fool is an enemy. We have to help him or send him to prison. If a friend sells drugs, we might be cool, but that fool is an enemy. Help him or get him locked. If our boy is paid, legally, but does not give at least 10% of his wealth and or time to save our community, we might be cool, but that fool is an enemy too. Before we can accept help from other communities we have to clean up our own house.

Compassionate warriors think outside of the box

To cut down internal foes we need to stop getting herded into the obvious intellectual ghettos. These are the places where we have the same simple minded recycled theories for the state of Black America.

The first intellectual ghetto is where we choose sides. Conservative? Liberal. For or against? It ain't that simple. Right is right. No matter your religion, race, or gender, right just feels right. You know it when you see it and feel it when you don't. The problem is when we start off by picking teams.

Once we choose sides we start to believe that all of the things that our team does are good and what their team does is bad. So Rush Limbaugh is always right if you're a conservative, but if you're a liberal he is the devil. Well, that's just stupid. Even our best friends say things that we disagree with. Therefore, we have to accept that even the most ridiculous amongst us gets lucky and says something that makes sense.

The second intellectual ghetto is our unresolved issues surrounding gender identity. For too many Black men our focus is on being unapologetic, cavemen. Unmodeled manhood is very dangerous. We can become so focused on being what our mothers told us men were supposed to be that we forget to be human. Our mothers were basing their definition on what our fathers didn't do and we try to deliver. We want to be as far away from being seen to be acting like women that we pretend to be unsympathetic and decisive, oh and, did I say right all of the time?

What if we could be human first? What if we could let that man mess go for a minute and we opened up to living simply as humans. You know, fumble with some questions, see the other side, and even be willing to learn from the other side, even if the other side is a woman. What if we started to redefine manhood? What if we sidestepped our paralyzing homophobia and just worked on being human, thoughtful and considerate? Then we would be free of the intellectual ghetto of one-dimensional manhood. We could live like humans and love unconditionally.

The third intellectual ghetto is the blame game. The horror of our community's challenges is so devastating that we believe that it has to be someone else's fault. For so many of us we have to believe that there is no way that Black people could have done this to ourselves. Right?

Unfortunately, placing the entire responsibility for the state of Black America on White people is like blaming the bed at night for stubbing our toe. Racism, like the dark that put the bed in our path, is the culprit, not the bed or the entire race.

It is without question that racists have always had help destroying us. Today Black people will kill more Black people than any other group will. We have to love our community enough to point out that it is walking around with toilet tissues sticking out of its pants. We must correct ourselves. Correction is among the highest forms of love so we must love ourselves to correct each other.

It's not just racism

Focusing solely or even primarily on White people, as the ongoing source of our failures, is simply immature. Black people run many of the communities that we live in. We are the elected officials, educators and preachers in these communities. Some of these communities are so Black that we have to import White kids to desegregate our schools. Sure these cities are broke. The industry has absolutely left, but jobs left poor White communities too. Get over it. What are we gonna do now, open another church?

When we sit back and take the scraps, we will never be given anything more. Black Americans have impacted every national election since John F. Kennedy and our absence from the voting booths guarantees that we will get the short end of the political stick. Drug sentencing, school funding, health care, affirmative action all will surely become casualties of our unwillingness to act politically. When we don't vote, we are tying the noose, standing under the tree and waiting for the inevitable. Regular Black men are not afraid of the system. They seek to correct it. Voting is one way. Blaming is what children do. Men find solutions.

Some White people are evil racists, but so are some Black people. Most White people could care less one way or the other about anyone other than themselves. That's just how PEOPLE are. There are gaps in what we know about each other. Sure, this can lead to conflict. But does this therefore mean that because Blacks and Whites are largely ignorant toward each other that all Black people are good?

People who are in control are not let off the hook. Let's get that straight. Every single one who challenges affirmative action with some tired arguments of reverse racism is simply trying to roll back the slim victories of our ancestors. They always find some sorry house Negro who so badly wants to be invited to massa's table that he will squash his own freedom. These people and their practices are easy to spot. You know where they are coming from and we are equipped to get after them. Tax cuts to the rich, deregulation of the FCC; this is the vernacular of the classism and racism. There is little sophistication in this so it is easy to spot.

C'mon. People *is* people, remember? Dumb people do dumb things. Racist people do racist things. Hustlers, hustle, rapists rape, lazy people don't work, talkers talk, and the world keeps spinning. There is no Santa Claus, Easter Bunny or organized White cartel. There isn't even a boogieman. There are people, some who want answers, and others who want someone to blame. Which one are you?

It's not all about the Benjamins

We need courageous Black men who do not define success in dollar signs. A rich life is one that enriches the lives of others, not one that pads the pockets of the liver. There is nothing wrong with money. Let's get that straight. A reward for hard effective work is cash compensation. Socialism is a fascinating concept and a very bad way to run a country. There is much that exists between socialism and unadulterated money grubbing. Defining a successful life by how much money we've made is at the core of our struggle.

Too many of us think that cash alone will cement the foundation of our future. That's simply false. The pursuit of money is just like any other. Chasing it comes to define us. It colors our days, casts our relationships and if unchecked, can become an addiction. When we define success by the size of our check, we start to work too long and leave our kids to be raised by somebody else. We miss the simple stuff that makes life productive. If we're good at something that we love, the money will come.

We fall down, but we get up

Regular Black men think Jesse Jackson has a point, but get tired of him trying to sell it. We feel that if we hear another Black Republican discount race as an issue, while wading in the kiddy pool of their party, we are gonna vomit. We don't feel comfortable being labeled as the talented tenth, but we also need to be validated for the years that we spend getting our butts kicked by both Blacks, who say we want to be White, and Whites who say we are too Black.

Regular Black men ain't poor enough to be Black or rich enough to be White. We've got White friends and relatives. Sometimes we live in the 'hood, but even when we don't, we have not forgotten it and the complex relationship that we have with it.

We are trying to reconcile sending our kids to an all White school. We watch the news with hands clasped in hopes that the bank robber, car jacker, abusive husband and D.C. sniper are not really Black.

We suffer in silence as our relatives accuse us of being uppity. We slap away White people's "compliments" that proclaim that 'you're so articulate'. We understand why White people are afraid of us and why Black people don't trust White people. We question brothers who date only White girls as we live with our Black wife and the memories of a few White girls of our past.

We have tasted the sweetness of academic and professional success. We struggle in these all White environments doing all we can to get a brother hired. Then we feel responsible every time he comes in late, talks to his baby's mother on the phone or works his butt off to get so close to the White people that he doesn't have ten minutes to let us know that he's got our back.

We are tired of Black people who can't dance and White folks who expect all of us to be able to. We've thrown a few 'affectionate' niggas ourselves, but can't stand to hear rappers hand them out to White people like Halloween candy. We count the number of Black people on the "Apprentice" and have had it up to here with BET. We know Tisha Campbell -Martin is on TV because she's light skinned and not because she's cute, yet none of us has a dark-skinned wife to take to this year's Junetenth gala.

Publicly we declare that Michael Steele, Lieutenant Governor of Maryland, is a sell-out but we will only agree privately with Al Sharpton. Tiger Woods is Black. Halle Berry did look silly crying like that at the Academy Awards. Denzel should have won the Oscar a decade ago for *Glory.*

When we're at home we occasionally watch "Jerry Springer" to see ugly women defiantly rip their tops off. Then we ask ourselves why. We admire Martin Luther King , Jr. and Hugh Hefner for the same reasons.

We sin throughout the day and get home in time to lead grace for dinner. We've loved hard and broken more hearts than laws. We are romantic when inspired and dutiful when pushed.

We are in love with a woman so much that we take her for granted. We forget. We forget how much we love her and how to tell her. We forget to pick up the toilet paper at the store and to refill the roll at home. We forget that we are married on business trips. We forget she's watching when we dote over our pets and kids and don't realize that this is all that she wants. We give what is easy to give and never an ounce more.

We are right most of the time. We can twist words together like Mr. Softie swirls a cone. We fight to win and will accept that her heart can be a casualty. We are self centered, egotistical and without flaws. We value work over the warmth of spooning on the couch. The remote control protrudes from our hands like fingernails and we can flip through 400 channels in two minutes and two seconds without looking down or missing the return of the game.

We have a few close friends that we have known forever. We trust some of them and we're okay with that. We think all of her friends are jealous.

Yes, our boys will provide cover for a jaunt to a strip club, bar or the arms of another, then they'll get us back in time to make sure that we don't allow the whiff of another to erase the commitment that we made to you the day after the wild bachelor party that they threw for us.

We are publicly emotionless, while privately we tear watching *Rudy* and *Remember the Titans*. We want to be strong even when strength is in short supply. We want you to look at us as your daddy, but want to make it clear that we ain't your father.

Sometimes things get complicated for regular Black men. Sometimes work gets in the way of home, home interferes with work, friends are all that we have and too much. Women give us purpose and cause us strife, fatherhood makes sense and we too often feel like we are doing it wrong.

We miss being single and dread being 40, in a club and

single. We have more than our parents and still feel like children when we are around them. We feel the pull of a community that is struggling to exist as we struggle among them.

It's life in all of its fuzzy glory. It is life that makes things feel so complicated. It's the process of living. It's the dash between our date of birth and death. It's the desire to help and the experience of being made to feel guilty for what we have by those we are trying to help. It's too much. It's not enough. It is life.

It's complicated trying to live up to expectations for which there are no applicable paradigms. Jesus and Allah sit on one shoulder and the devil lounges on the other. It's complicated untangling feelings of elation and debauchery, especially when they come from the same activity. Even being regular is complicated, simply because being regular means dealing with life, instead of checking out. It means seeing and accepting our roles even when we have no idea what responding to them entails.

What is most important about us is that we want and need to do right more often than not. We believe in God, family, the Black community, friends of all nations and our country. We accept the responsibility of the race. We get the holocaust. We know that we are outnumbered in and out of our community. Sure there are more of us in jail than college, but we still believe.

We know that the world is expected of us. We feel the heat of responsibility burning our necks. Its rays follow us through our days and light our nights. We feel inadequate and overqualified. When we stand in front of the mirror each morning to shave, we set out to do so much good.

We live in the inconsistency of our desires. We fall short and exceed expectations. We raise the bar and forget there was one. We are everything that you hoped for and all that you never dreamed you would have to contend with.

We are trifling, this is true, but we ultimately come through. Our greatest strength is that we get it. We understand that we stand at the foot of our collective destiny and in the face of adversity.

We will go to work all of the time. We will provide for the family, all of the time. We will struggle with expressing our emotions all of the time. We will come home, all of the time.

We will forget the nuances of life. The things that warm the heart of a sister will slip past us like a burglar in the night, but when you need us, even if we are late, we will be there. We will finish the job that you started. We will read the kids stories tonight, take the garbage off the porch to the curb, carry the clothes to the dryer, and buy you something the night before our anniversary.

Loving a regular Black man will not cost you the house, a car, trips to the pen, but it may cost you your sanity. With us in your life you will grow stronger. You will enjoy the simple pleasures of fighting over the color of a room, chores, money, sex, in-laws, listening and talking too much. These are the sparks that will keep the fires going. They will ignite questions of why we are together. As these questions are answered our union will be renewed. Like a muscle that tears from the stress of a hard workout, our bond will only grow stronger. The regularity of our struggles to understand each other will make us stronger. There will be no flat streets on our journey to forever, but through it all you will know deep down that, whether together or apart, we ultimately want the same thing, to improve our little piece of the community.

What is special about regular Black men is that we will fall down, but we will get up. We have enough pride to want to be better each day. We know ultimately that Black men do not have the luxury to be regular. We always have to be more, more than just a father, brother, son, husband, boyfriend, employee, preacher or man.

A regular Black man acknowledges his responsibilities, hunting them down like prey. Galloping through the brush of the New World he gives chase. He knows that the community needs him to capture the agile prey. As it shifts and darts in and out of the institutions of our existence, a regular Black man tears after his responsibilities. He knows that he cannot let them graze in the fields of this hostile place alone. He has to grab hold of his responsibilities and bring them back to his lair. He uses all of his wit, skill, energy and drive to deliver his completed responsibilities. His days are spent plotting against the odds and the elements. When he misses, tumbling for yards, he gathers himself, settles back in and when responsibility appears again, his ears perk, his lids raise, back straightens and within seconds he is off again, compelled by duty to complete his responsibility of being a responsible regular Black man.

A regular Black man falls down, but he will never stay down. Rise up brothers. Stand tall. Man up because nobody is coming to save us. Begin.

...okay, now what?

The hardest part about writing this book is being held to the standards therein. I am just as guilty of some of the negative behaviors outlined in this book as those I call out. I'm a regular Black man who is living and making mistakes every day. I am there with you as you try to encourage people to do their share to improve the community while trying to avoid being a hypocrite.

Unlike you I now have a living record of what I think Black men, and the women who love us, need to do to make things better. As you've seen, I've criticized people that I think are coming up short. Then I demanded that everybody look into themselves FIRST for solutions, then I do the opposite. I tell you what to do then I talk about myself. If this isn't hypocrisy, then I don't know what is. Even as I try to avoid being a hypocrite, I am one..... so now what?

I, like you, keep trying. I keep trying to make contributions to our community that are thoughtful and long lasting. If you'd like to join me in my imperfect journey, I sure could use the help.

Biography

Steve Perry is the author of two other books of fiction, *The Window Pain* and *Naked Eating Chinese Food*. Both focus on Black men's development and relationships.

Perry is the founder and principal of The Capital Preparatory Magnet School in Hartford, CT. Capital Prep is a grade six through twelve college preparatory school with a focus on social justice. Its students are largely Black and Latino and from Hartford. The remaining students are from fifteen other cities and towns in Greater Hartford. Prior to starting the school Perry was the founder and director of the Capital ConnCAP Collaborative, a state and privately funded Upward Bound program that sent 100% of its graduates to college.

The fire that started in the heart of Steve Perry began when he was as a child born to a teen mother living in public housing. It still rages in the man. This fire is the source of his inspiration to write and seek to educate the community's children.

Steve Perry's commitment to the community began long before he received his masters in social work from the University of Pennsylvania. Even as an undergraduate, he proved that there is more than one road to take to empower the community. Whether working for a US Senator, mayor or presidential candidate as an undergraduate at the University of Rhode Island, or later while serving as director of a homeless shelter, Steve has explored many facets of community empowerment.

Perry has been a Democratic candidate for state representative and a community college adjunct professor, while at the same time serving on numerous regional and local boards.

References

Allen, J. As a man Thinketh. New York, NY Grosse & Dunlop
(ISBN 0-399-12829-8).

Avery, C. M. (2001). Teamwork is and individual skill. San
Francisco, Barrett-Koehler Publishers (ISBN 1-57675-
155-4).

Bolman, L.G. & Deal, T.E (1997). Reframing organizations:
Artistry, choice and leadership, 3rd edition. San
Francisco, Jossey-Bass Publishers (ISBN 0-7879-
6426-3).

Bickel, R., Howley, C., Williams, T. and Glascock, C. (2001,
October 8). High School Size, Achievement Equity, and
Cost: Robust Interaction Effects and Tentative Results.
Education Policy Analysis Archives, 9(40). Retrieved
Policy Analysis Archives, 10(32). Retrieved [September
28, 2003] from http://epaa.asu.edu/epaa/v10n32/.

Caldwell, R. (2003). Change leaders and change managers:
different or complimentary. Birkbeck College, University
of London, London, UK.

Center for Disease Control. Healthy youth! Retrieved [January 8,
2005] from http://apps.nccd.cdc.gov/YRBSS/index.asp.

Comer, J. P. (2004). Leaving no child behind: Preparing today's
youth for tomorrow's world, New Haven & London
Yale University Press (ISBN 0-300-103991-3).

Clinchy, E. (2000). Creating new schools: How small schools are
changing American education. New York, NY, Teachers
College Press (ISBN 0-8077-3876-X).

Donaldson, G. Jr. (2001). Cultivating leadership in schools:

Connecting people, purpose, and practice. New York, NY, Teachers College Press (ISBN 0-8077-4002-0).

Dudley, R. (1971). The black poets. New York, NY, Bantam Books (ISBN 0-553-27563-1).

Dyson, M. E. (2003). Open Mike. New York, NY, Basic Civitas Books (ISBN 0-465-01765-7).

Epps, A. (1991). Malcolm X speeches at Harvard. New York, NY, Paragon House (ISBN 1-55778-479-5).

Ferrero, D. J. (2003, August 25). Embracing Pedagogical Pluralism: An Educator's Case for (at Least Public) School Choice. Education Policy Analysis Archives, 11(30). Retrieved [September 28, 2003] from http://epaa.asu.edu/epaa/v11n30/.

Fullan, M. (2003). Change forces with a vengeance. New York, Rutledge Falmer (ISBN 0-415-2308-3).

Fullan, M. (2001). Change forces the sequel. New York, Rutledge Falmer (ISBN 0-7507-0755-0).

Frankenberg, E. and Lee, C. (2003, September 5). Charter schools and race: A lost opportunity for integrated education. Education Policy Analysis Archives, 11(32). Retrieved [September 28, 2003] from http://epaa.asu.edu/epaa/v11n32.

Linton, T. H. & Kester, D. (2003, March 14). Exploring the achievement gap between white and minority students in Texas: A comparison of the 1996 and 2000 NAEP and TAAS eighth grade mathematics test results, Education Policy Analysis Archives, 11(10). Retrieved [October 20, 2003] from http://epaa.asu.edu/epaa/v11n10/.

Harris, F. (1996). A case study of an interdistrict magnet 1996.

University of Hartford.Interdistrict Magnet School Planning Guide, September 2001, Bureau of Equity and Choice, CT State Department of Education.

Huy, Q. & Mintzberg, H. (2003). The rhythm of change. MIT Sloan Management School, Cambridge MA.

Jurnal of Pediatrics (August 2003). African American and Teen Mothers Have a Greater Risk for Low-birth Weight and Premature Babies. Baltimore, MD Johns Hopkins Bloomberg School of Public Health. Retrieved [September 10, 2005] from http://www.jhsph.edu/ CHN/Resources/riskfactors.html.

Kouzes, J. & Posner, B. (1999). Encouraging the heart. San Francisco, Jossey-Bass Publishers (ISBN 0-7879-6426-3).

Maehr, M. L. & Midgley, C. (1996). Transforming school cultures. Westview Press, Bolder, CO. (ISBN 0-8133-2743-1).

National Assocaition of Black Journalists, official website Retrieved [January 10, 2005] http://www.nabj.org/

National Assocaition of Black MBAs, official website Retrieved [January 10, 2005] http://www.nbmbaa.org/

National Assocaition of Black Social Workers, official website Retrieved [January 10, 2005] fromhttp:// www.nabsw.org/mserver/Default.aspx

Kennard, J. Statistics Show African American Men Worse off. Men's Health Retrieved [September 10, 2005] from http://menshealth.about.com/od/blackhealth/a/ Af_amer_stats.htm.

King, M. (1963). Letter from a Birmingham jail. Retrieved

[September 28, 2005] from http://www.sas.upenn.edu/ African_Studies/Articles_Gen/Letter_Birmingham.html.

Smrekar, C. & Goldering, E. (1999). School choice in urban America: Magnet schools and the pursuit of equity. New York, NY, Teachers College Press (ISBN 0-8077-38728-X).

Sykes, T. (2005). Black Enterprise. Vol. 36. Issue 1. New York, NY

Thernstrom, A & S. (2003). No excuses. New York, NY, Simon & Schuster (ISBN 0-7432-0446-8).

Walker, E. M. (2002, August 4). The politics of school-based management: Understanding the process of devolving authority in urban school districts. Education Policy Analysis Archives, 10(33). Retrieved [September 28, 2003] from http://epaa.asu.edu/epaa/v10n33.html.

Woodson, C. (1933). The mi-education of the Negro.Chicago, Ill (ISBN 0-913543-70-5).

Wheatley, M. (2002). Turning to one another: Simple conversations to restore hope to the future. San Francisco, Barrett-Koehler (ISBN 1-57675-145-7).